Writing for Interaction

Writing for Interaction

Crafting the Information Experience for Web and Software Apps

Linda Newman Lior

Light-Wise Information Experience Design (light-wise.com)

AMSTERDAM • BOSTON • HEIDELBERG • LONDON
NEW YORK • OXFORD • PARIS • SAN DIEGO
SAN FRANCISCO • SINGAPORE • SYDNEY • TOKYO
Morgan Kaufmann is an imprint of Elsevier

ELSEVIER

Acquiring Editor: *Meg Dunkerley*
Development Editor: *Heather Scherer*
Project Manager: *Malathi Samayan*
Designer: *Mark Rogers*

Morgan Kaufmann is an imprint of Elsevier
225 Wyman Street, Waltham, MA 02451, USA

Library of Congress Cataloging-in-Publication Data

Lior, Linda Newman.
   Writing for interation : crafting the information experience for Web and software Apps / Dr. Linda Newman Lior.
      pages cm
   Includes bibliographical references and index.
   ISBN 978-0-12-394813-7 (pbk.)
   1. User interfaces (Computer systems) 2. Web-based user interfaces. 3. Application software--Development 4. Website development. I. Title.
   QA76.9.U83L56 2013
   005.4'37--dc23
                                                2013001111

British Library Cataloguing-in-Publication Data
A catalogue record for this book is available from the British Library.

ISBN: 978-0-12-394813-7

Contents

Acknowledgments

Writing a book is much like raising a child. There's the joy when things go well, the trepidation and worry when things are faltering, the exhaustion of long days and nights, and an overwhelming sense of satisfaction in having accomplished what once seemed impossible. And like a child, it takes nothing less than a small village to succeed. I couldn't have written this book without my village of supporters, who knowingly or unknowingly guide, encourage, and inspire me every day.

My deepest gratitude to my colleagues, past and present, with whom I have spent countless hours working and collaborating, and learning from, throughout the years, in particular: Yoshua Idar, Adina Hagege, Nathan Bigman, Rayne Wiselman, Vladimir Holostov, Debi Parush, Sara Tzadok, Michelle Friedman, Claire Brosh, Eilon Reshef , and Yonatan Zamir (along with the rest of my Microsoft, LaHit, and Webcollage teams).

Thank you to my reviewers—Rayne Wiselman, Mark Magee, and Sharon Ainspan—for their timely and thoughtful input; to David Farbey, Saul Carliner, Sharon Ainspan, and Yossi Avnon for the materials they provided; and to the wonderful people from Elsevier—Rachel Roumeliotis, Heather Sherer, and Meg Dunkerly—for getting me through the process.

Thank you to my dear friends—Ellen Cohen for getting me into the book-writing business to begin with, and Rayne Wiselman whose insightful feedback and practical advice have guided me in so many ways. And thank you to my everlasting friends on both continents for their love and encouragement throughout the years.

Special thanks and acknowledgments to my wonderful family—my four Lior men—Omri, Ariel, Yarden, and Gilad—my parents Albert and Shirley Newman, Elisa Newman White, Rozzi Newman Osterman, Haya Ben-Yacov, and the rest of the Lior/Newman/Lample family for their never-ending support and love.

About The Author

Linda Newman Lior has been working on the design and development of software for over 20 years in the field of information design. Her experience includes instructional design for educational software programs and computer-based training, information design for start-up companies, and 10 years at Microsoft as a usability engineer, information experience designer, and technical writer. She is currently focusing on information experience design and writing for SaaS web applications. She studied instructional design and computers in education at San Diego State University where she earned her MA in Educational Technology.

Introduction

This book is about designing and creating the content your customers rely on for successfully interacting with your application. This content appears in a variety of forms and formats, serving a variety of purposes—from the labels on each button your customers click on to initiate an action to the step-by-step instructions displayed on the pages of your application.

This book introduces the processes and strategies you need to provide the content to your customers as the "information experience." As the term *content* implies, it's more than a combination of letters and words: Rather, each word, sentence, instruction, and message appearing within the user interface should contribute to the overall understanding and successful interaction between your customers and the technology behind the user interface.

This book describes how you can design, create, and deliver the information experience for your application, and discusses its impact and importance as an integral component of the application and user experience.

WHO IS THIS BOOK FOR?

When I started writing this book, I assumed the audience would be primarily technical writers and instructional designers who were interested in improving or expanding their skill-set by writing user interface text. As the book progressed, however, I came to understand that as teams struggle to keep up with delivery schedules on minimal headcounts, it's often the developers, product managers, and user experience designers who are tasked with creating the text within the user interface. As such, this book is for anyone who finds they are writing, editing, or reviewing the user interface text, and all that it entails.

What Will You Learn from Reading This Book?

The impulse to put everything into a book is difficult to suppress. However, there are only so many pages a reader wants in a single book and just so many pages a writer can provide. This book presents the processes, concepts, and guidelines that will help you design, deliver, and create a successful information experience for your customers.

It's not a book on user experience design, nor is it a book that teaches writing and grammar. This book will teach you the strategies and processes for creating information that bridges the gap between static writing and user experience design, and in so doing, it will provide the information users need for interacting with your application.

How to Read This Book

While you don't necessarily need to read this book in a specific order—and I doubt you will read it from end to end as you would a novel—it was designed to present the information as a process.

- Section 1 provides an overview of the concept of the information experience and traces its evolultion. The section also describes the impact of the information experience on the overall end-user experience. It also describes how to integrate your processes into the team process and the interaction between the information writer and the rest of the roles making up the team.
- Section 2 describes how to gather data about your customers and how to use the data to understand their information needs. It also explains how to create target personas, and how these personas help keep the end user's needs at the center of your information strategy.
- Section 3 covers the concepts and strategies you need for designing your content based on how users read and interact with content, and on the information needs of your customers. It also describes how to create the guidelines you will use to produce content that is consistent, clear, and concise.
- Section 4 shows how you develop and create the content based on usability principles and writing guidelines.
- Section 5 describes how to evaluate the information experience created using Section 4, so that you can improve and revise it as needed.

The screen samples provided in this book are designed to show both the positive and less positive examples of user interface text and information, These samples come from a variety of sources found online in Internet applications and in operating systems. I apologize to the writers of any of these pages described as anything less than favorable. Any visuals that were not released to the public are used with permission.

This book is the culmination of my years of studying education and instructional design at San Diego State University and 25 years of my experience working in the realms of instructional designer, technical writer and usability engineer on dozens of applications, and with countless numbers of product managers, project managers, technical writers and editors, developers, testers, user experience designers, graphic artists, and end users, all of whom have taught me something along the way. There are many good books on the market today describing each of these realms. Because the underlying principles behind these disciplines overlap, some sections in this book may be similar to content presented in other books; any such similarities are simply a result of overlapping disciplines, and are not intentional.

Introducing *Writing for Interaction*

Welcome to *Writing for Interaction*.

Creating software and web applications requires collaboration and coordination between teams and groups, each working toward the common goal of providing the best possible user experience for their customers.

While some product features and development roles, such as programmer, are clearly defined, the information users interact with and rely on for using your application, and the role of writing that information are less well understood.

This section introduces the concept of the information experience and how the flow of information provided within the user interface impacts how your customers interact with your application and their overall perception of the user experience. It also describes the components of the information ecosystem and how the information experience is part of that ecosystem. The chapter also discusses the difference between writing for web sites and writing for web applications.

Because teams use development models and processes to create applications, the section describes the various models used by most software development teams. It describes user- centered design (UCD) as the basis for keeping your customers at the forefront of application design. Finally, the section describes the importance of team collaboration and how the role of information experience designer interacts with the rest of the team, to create a successful information experience for your users.

CHAPTER 1

Introducing the Information Experience

INTRODUCTION

Ever since computer applications became widely used in offices and homes, the need for information supporting these applications has grown. At the same time, the need for professionals who provide this information has also evolved. The skills required by these professionals have also changed to meet the needs of the people who use these applications.

Consumers of today's software and web applications want, and expect, applications to be easy to navigate and understand within the context of the tasks they are trying to complete. In this model, information is not for passive consumption; rather, users interact with the information as they work with the application—entering data and making selections and decisions. The information users encounter must be delivered in a way that is easy to find and to understand and appears at the right time.

Whether you're a product manager, developer, designer, technical writer, or an experienced information architect, creating a positive information experience takes careful planning, patience, and good writing skills. The processes, guidelines, and practical examples provided in this book are designed to help you hone your writing skills to create positive, interactive information experiences that will delight consumers of your applications.

WHAT IS THE INFORMATION EXPERIENCE?

In a world where people of all ages and backgrounds are spending increasingly more of their work and leisure time navigating through software and web applications, the information they encounter and interact with along the way is key to their ability to enjoy and use these applications. In this quickly evolving technical world, where applications are now available and used across a multitude of platforms and devices, delivery systems for this information are also evolving. Whereas traditionally information was delivered via a user manual and help system, today applications require a complete information ecosystem that goes hand in hand with the application. In this ecosystem, information is an integral part of an application and the overall end-user experience.

The integration and interaction between the application, the user experience, and the information ecosystem are what forms the *information experience*.

Information Experience Workflow

The information created for each product depends on many factors, such as the knowledge level of the user, the complexity of the product, and the user tasks and workflow. A successful information experience goes hand in hand with the user experience, providing the textual cues and instructions users need to successfully navigate the system.

Software versus Web Applications

Whether you are writing for a software package or a web application, the information you provide has a goal: to help users successfully interact with your application for the purpose of completing tasks.

Let's imagine a typical workflow one user may follow to install and run a software application. In this example, our user is Steve, who works in a small business. Steve's boss asks him to set up the new software application the company will use for tracking expenses. Since Steve isn't a computer professional, he's somewhat nervous about this task, but he's determined to get everything running smoothly so that he can impress his boss.

1. Steve opens the box, and reads the release notes and installation requirements accompanying the application CD.
2. He inserts the CD into the computer and opens the step-by-step installation guide. The Setup program automatically displays, and Steve follows the instructions on each page of the Setup wizard, referring to the corresponding page in the Installation Guide as he goes along.
3. After Setup completes, Steve picks up the user manual. He turns to the Getting Started section and follows the instructions to log into the application and open the console. Once the console opens, Steve is relieved to see that a Quick Configuration wizard is already open in the console.
4. Steve goes through the Quick Configuration wizard, using the descriptions and labels in the wizard pages to select the settings he needs.

The help links, available on each wizard page, are useful for helping him understand the implications of the settings.

5. The final page in the wizard lists the settings that will be saved and applied when Steve clicks Finish on the final page of the wizard. When the settings are saved, a message appears, letting Steve know that the settings were successfully saved.

6. Next Steve wants to configure the application according to the team's requirements. Steve starts by looking around in the user interface for the settings he wants. He also opens the online help and searches for keywords that will lead him to the right settings.

7. Steve finds the topic he needs in the help, and follows the instructions in the topic. He navigates to the property pages he needs. The tab titles make it easy for him to find the settings he is looking for, and the text prompts and inline instructions guide him. Steve selects the options he needs and saves the settings.

8. Next, Steve logs into the product web site and registers the product. He also joins the product newsgroup on the product portal. He looks through the comments and blogs. When he has a question, this is where he will post it.

9. Later, Steve wants to understand more about how the program works. He looks through the user manual to read about monitoring the system and to learn about additional features he may want to configure later.

This is an example of a positive information experience. At each step, Steve's interactions with the information help him complete the process successfully and efficiently.

For web applications, the experience and expectations are somewhat different: Users come from a wider range of computer skills, ages, backgrounds, abilities, and motivation levels. They expect to log in, get set up, and get going with little or no formal documents. And since many of these services are free, at least during the initial trial period, it's crucial to get users over the learning curve as quickly as possible, or risk them moving on to an easier-to-use application.

In the next example, Steve is now at his home computer and decides to use an online home finance application to keep track of family finances.

1. Steve searches the Internet to find the service he is looking for. He clicks into the web site and starts to navigate around the site looking for useful information.

2. Steve watches a short video describing the benefits of this application and another video providing an overview of how it works. He reads a few quotes from satisfied users. He notices that a page containing

instructional videos and documents about the system are available. Then he clicks the Get Started Now button.

3. Steve is prompted to create an account by entering a user name and password. After setting up his account, the application opens and a short tutorial displays, showing him the steps he'll follow to get started.

4. Steve watches the tutorial and is ready to start entering information. He notices that the Accounts page is displayed, just as the tutorial explained.

5. Steve begins filling in the details about his savings and checking accounts into the web page. The drop-down menu items and text boxes are clearly labeled. The captions and prompts on the page make it easy to understand what information is required. When Steve is not sure what to fill in, he clicks on the related help link, which provides a short explanation and examples.

6. After entering his account details, Steve clicks the Expenses tab and begins entering his expenses into the page. The layout of the page and provided examples make it easy for him to understand how to enter his expenses. Help links are available when he needs additional information to understand the field.

7. When he's done entering the information, Steve clicks the Save button, and a message confirming his data was saved is provided. Steve is satisfied and closes the application for the day. He plans to update the information every evening.

In this example, the information experience is well integrated into the user experience, providing Steve with the information he needs, when and where he needs it. Steve understood right away what the application could do for him, how to get started, and what he needed to do to enter his data. Ideally, all applications should be this simple to understand and use.

At each step in both of the above examples, there was also a chance for failure. If Steve hadn't found the information he needed, if the user interface hadn't provided the right prompts, and if he hadn't been able to understand how to complete the task at hand, he would have been frustrated and unhappy, and, he may have been unable to complete the process.

By creating a positive information experience, you can help ensure that users like Steve are successful and satisfied customers of the applications you help create.

Web Application versus Web Sites

While it's often difficult to tell the difference between a web site and a web application, the content required for each is very different. Web sites are designed for advertising or marketing a company or service, or for providing information about specific topics. Content for web sites is written mainly for passive consumption; interactive text is for helping users navigate through the pages of the site and for a limited set of activities such as creating an account and completing forms.

Web applications, on the other hand, are designed for completing tasks. Your text in a web application is for educating and guiding users in successfully completing tasks and actions. Many web sites provide a download link, requiring users to download a client component for using the web application. For example, skype.com provides access to the Skype web application, but it also serves as the company's portal to the outside world. In cases like this, while the web site provides many interactive elements, its primary purpose is to inform and sell its products and services. Skype.com is a web site, which is separate from Skype, which is a web application.

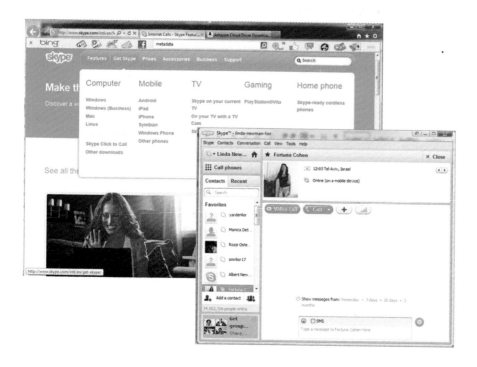

Content in a web site is written for marketing and informational purposes, while the text in the application is for helping users interact with and successfully complete tasks.

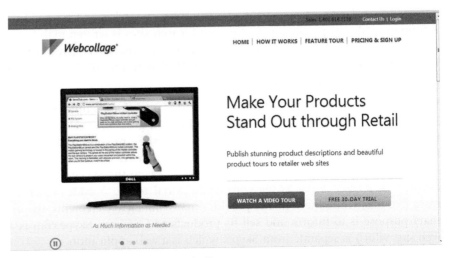

FIGURE 1.1 Example of a product web site.

Not all web applications require users to download a component, but they may have a separate management console users log into for completing their tasks.

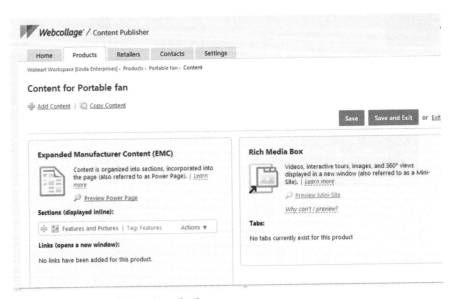

FIGURE 1.2 The product web application.

In contrast to web applications, web services don't usually require users to download a client component or log into a console to complete their tasks. The user accesses the application over the Internet and uses it remotely from a desktop or other device. Users don't usually distinguish between a web application and a web service; as such, there are no significant differences in writing interactive content between the two.

Where a difference does come into play is that companies providing a web service often use the site to advertise their other available products and to inform users about their services. In this case, striking the balance between instructional writing and marketing writing is challenging and requires different skills. In the following example, users create an account, learn how to use the application, and can become familiar with the company all on the same site.

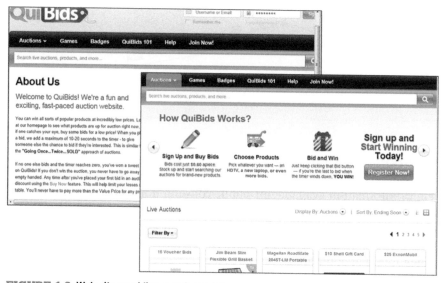

FIGURE 1.3 Web site providing a web service

Web applications come in a variety of categories, each with its distinct look and feel, and content needs. Understanding the primary purpose and tasks of the application will help you provide the right information experience for your users.

Components of an Information Ecosystem

The term *information ecosystem* was traditionally used to describe an entire system of information available for public consumption, such as television and radio broadcasts, newspapers, magazines, and other widely distributed media. In the context of a software or web application, the information ecosystem includes all the information supporting, provided with, and integrated into that application.

Just as the components comprising an application must be planned to fit together seamlessly, the information ecosystem, together with its integration into the application it supports, requires the same kind of planning. In addition, the information delivery mechanisms must develop in the same direction as the technology it supports. Even a single application may have a variety of delivery mechanisms based on the delivery platform.

Let's take a look at each component of the information ecosystem and its place within the information experience.

FIGURE 1.4 Main components of the information ecosystem.

Print Materials

Software companies generally release their applications with accompanying print materials—most commonly in the form of user guides and installation guides. Depending on the complexity of the application and the skills of the users, there may be additional books, such as technical references and white papers. As the life of the product progresses, additional training materials and technical papers may be added to the documentation set.

When the first software programs were developed in the 1960s, the creators and consumers of the accompanying documents and guides were mainly programmers, engineers, or other highly skilled technical users. The documents were mostly procedural, and little attention was paid to formatting and fonts. When desktop computers starting making their way into companies and government offices in the United States, computers suddenly became a tool used by nontechnical workers who didn't speak the same language as the programmers. With this shift, well written, easy to read documentation became a necessity and paramount to the user's success.

Examples of printed documentation include

- User manuals and guides
- Technical references
- Getting Started booklets and Quick Start cards
- Technical white papers

When determining the number of documents and document types that are needed for creation of an application, it's important to understand the knowledge levels of the users, the complexity of the application, and the amount of information the user actually needs. It's also important to distinguish between active versus reactive content. Proactive content is content users seek out to complete a task or an action. Reactive content is content users need in reaction to a specific occurrence, such as a monitoring alert or a change to the system settings. Understanding user needs and the differences between proactive versus reactive content will be discussed in later chapters.

"In the Box" Help Systems

Although printed books and guides are a good resource for getting a system up and running, and for learning about the features of an application and how it works, they don't provide the information users need to complete a task or process within the context of the user workflow. In addition, as computers have become more mobile, print materials may not be within reach when information is needed.

The introduction of online help systems created a way to deliver nonlinear information as part of the application, providing "just-in-time" information within the context of the task at hand.

Depending on where the users are in a process, they can read online help one topic at a time or in sections. The addition of indexes and search capabilities provides even more flexibility, allowing users to search the content based on keywords or phrases.

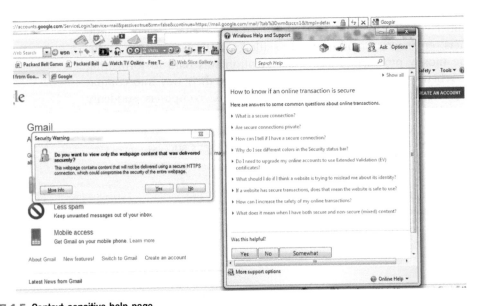

FIGURE 1.5 Context-sensitive help page.

The big push toward online help systems occurred in the 1990s when the creation of easy to use authoring tools, based on the compilation of individual files, made it possible for technical writers to create the content and compile it into a single help file, with programmers creating the hooks between the files comprising the help and the related screens in the user interface.

Examples of help systems shipped with an application

- Context-sensitive help integrated into the application
- Help panes opening html pages
- Compiled help file—users can search the help pages
- Tutorials

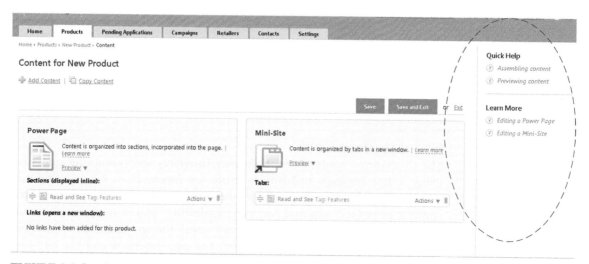

FIGURE 1.6 Sample context-sensitive help pane.

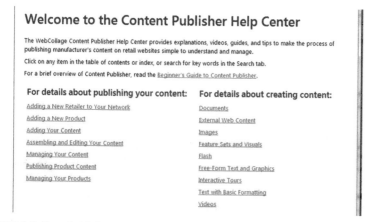

FIGURE 1.7 Compiled help center.

FIGURE 1.8 Getting Started Tutorial.

User Interface Text

The first computers had very little user interface, with computer operators using a few buttons and punch cards for input. Even when computers became available to the public in the 1970s, computer screens had little content, possessed minimal graphics capabilities, and were operated mainly using command line input. It wasn't until the graphical user interface (GUI) was created and developed that the user interface and the end-user experience became important. Suddenly, companies began investing in building "user friendly" applications, which required combining graphics and text.

FIGURE 1.9 Portable computer evolution (IBM, 1977–2012).

This led to new ways of providing information and creating interfaces that are intuitive and easy to learn and navigate. In addition, the information provided with these systems must also be easy to learn and navigate.

Examples of information within the user interface

- Getting Started instructions and tutorials
- Wizards with guided instructions
- Captions and labels (page titles, subtitles, and prompts)
- Error and status messages
- Inline explanatory text (e.g., notes, tooltips, and hover text)

With web, mobile, and home software applications reaching wider audiences, the impact of the content within the user interface has become increasingly more important. This requires careful crafting and design of the information to match the application and delivery mechanism.

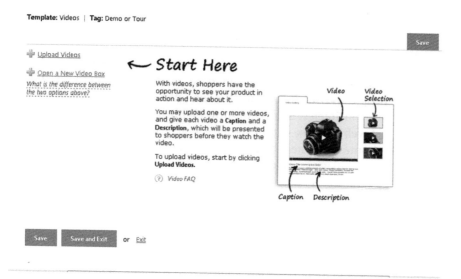

FIGURE 1.10 Example of instruction integrated in the user interface (web application).

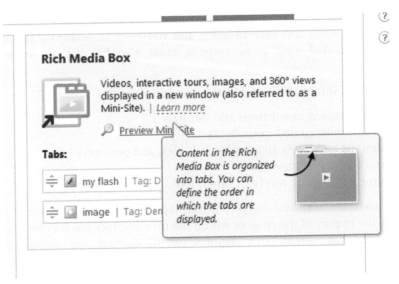

FIGURE 1.11 Inline help links.

Online (Web) Content

When the English computer scientist Tim Berners-Lee developed the World Wide Web, adding a graphical user interface (GUI) to the Internet way back in 1991, people who had never used a computer were able to interact with the Internet, and interest started to grow. With the release of Windows 3.1 and the first web browser within the next year, and then Windows 95 a few years later, home computers became mainstream and the information superhighway was on its way. Suddenly, anyone with a computer and an Internet connection had access to a world of information in a variety of formats, which could be viewed online or downloaded.

As the Internet became increasingly popular, business opportunities blossomed. In 1995, the concept of the web application was introduced and a new business model of software as a service (SaaS) was created. For software developers, SaaS demanded a new approach to software design and development. For information architects, the Internet provided a new platform for creating and distributing information. Instead of turning to print documents and online help systems provided in the box, users began relying exclusively on the inline text and searching the web for everything from marketing to troubleshooting information. In response to this shift, companies began using the Internet for distributing materials about their products on their company's web site and on cloud-based help portals.

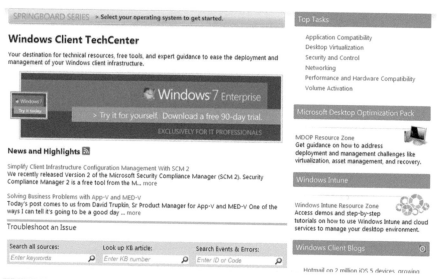

FIGURE 1.12 Example of a Windows product Internet help portal.

Examples of information distributed via the Internet

- "How to" articles, blogs, and videos
- Feature and product highlights
- Release notes and updates to existing documents
- Troubleshooting advice
- Marketing updates
- Technical information (e.g., white papers)

Information distributed via the Internet comes in a variety of delivery mechanisms and formats. Whether housed in an online content management system, such as a help portal, or directly on the company web site, the content of any number of content types may be derived, such as multimedia (videos), webinars, blogs, newsgroup posts, and downloadable documents.

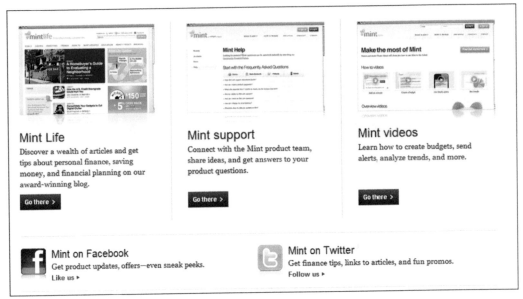

FIGURE 1.13 Example of an Internet application help portal page (on the product web site).

In addition, social networking applications, such as Facebook and Twitter, have become increasingly used for posting ongoing updates about products and events.

FIGURE 1.14 Content distributed using Facebook.

WHAT IS THE MOST SIGNIFICANT DIFFERENCE BETWEEN WRITING USER INTERFACE TEXT AND THE INFORMATION PROVIDED IN THE DOCUMENTATION OR OTHER COLLATERAL DOCUMENTS?

Saul Carliner, PhD, CTDP
Editor-in-Chief, IEEE Transactions on Professional Communication

The difference is similar to that of writing for web sites and web applications. Interface text is primarily intended to prompt users to do something. It needs to be sparse but provide sufficient guidance to help users figure out how to respond to a particular prompt. So the writing is terse, though clear. It might use jargon and technical terms, providing the author is certain that users are familiar with such terms.

But if a few words are too few to help users figure out how to respond, they need to turn to documentation and other collateral. In some cases, they need more detailed explanations than are appropriate in the interface. In other cases, they need hand-holding, demonstrations, and other types of assistance that go way beyond what's appropriate in an on-screen prompt in the interface.

Documentation is more explanatory; it should provide definitions of all technical jargon and terms, and often, examples. If the collateral is instructional, it also needs to provide opportunities to practice, receive feedback, and develop competence in a particular skill. The instructional material and feedback need to be written in a supportive way, which makes tone critical.

Saul Carliner, Director, Education Doctoral Program and Associate Professor, Concordia University, saulcarliner@hotmail.com, Blog: http://saulcarliner.blogspot.com

SUMMARY

Whether your application is distributed as a software package or as a web application, one of your greatest challenges will be defining the content types and delivery methods comprising the information ecosystem and information experience for your application. Learning how your users work with the application and being acquainted with their needs and the distribution mechanisms are crucial for creating and delivering the right information. And while the information ecosystem includes a variety of components, the most prevalent component for your users is the information within the user interface: This is the information users need to successfully interact with your application.

In later chapters, you will learn methods for evaluating user needs and creating your content.

- The integration between the components of the information ecosystem and the user experience form the *information experience*.
- The information ecosystem consists of print materials, user interface text, in-the-box help systems, and information provided on the web.

- A successful information experience provides information that is easy for users to find, navigate, understand, and interact with.
- When using an application, users are looking to complete tasks, and the content is for active interaction. Content for web sites follows many of the same guidelines as content for applications, but the user needs are different.[1]

---

[1]Several good books are available that can help you write web site content, for example, *Letting Go of the Words: Writing Web Content That Works* by Janice (Ginny) Reddish.

CHAPTER 2

Design and Development Models and Processes

INTRODUCTION

Whether your application is being developed by a large corporation or is the single application developed by a small start-up, teams need processes and mechanisms for designing and coding the features, as well as for creating and tracking development and release milestones. While large software teams may take years to develop and release a single application, other teams work in short cycles with multiple releases. Understanding the type of model your team uses helps you design and create your interface text by keeping in step with the rest of the team and the development cycle.

WHAT ARE DESIGN AND DEVELOPMENT MODELS?

Design and development models provide the framework for creating applications that meet user needs and requirements. Software teams also rely on development models to make sure realistic schedules are in place and that implementation milestones are defined. Whether you're working on a software or web application, when designing the information experience, it's important to understand how to integrate your milestones into the model and processes your team uses. At the same time, it is important to recognize that development schedules tend to be fluid and that flexibility is a key element of planning. While the overall development life cycle and the phases in each model may vary in emphasis, each approach uses similar phases and guiding principles.

User-Centered Design

User-centered design (UCD) is at the core of most modern software design processes. The main philosophy of user-centered design is that the needs, abilities, and wants of the end user drive the design at each stage of the process. User scenarios, personas, and requirements are created, evaluated, and considered from the beginning of the product life cycle. The information gathered at the early stages is used to define the product features and end-user experience. As the product design progresses, user testing and user input are used to refine the features.

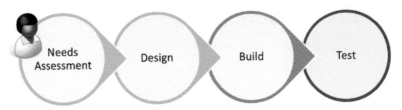

FIGURE 2.1 User-centered design model.

UCD is implemented as part of the overall development model. At each stage, the product team considers user needs and how those needs can be met.

The shift toward UCD has led to user experience and information experience design that is based on user workflows rather than on the product features. Information within the user experience, such as informative text, labels, and inline help links—as well as the content and structure of accompanying help systems and documentation—are designed to follow the same considerations, matching user workflows to how users complete tasks rather than to how users configure features.

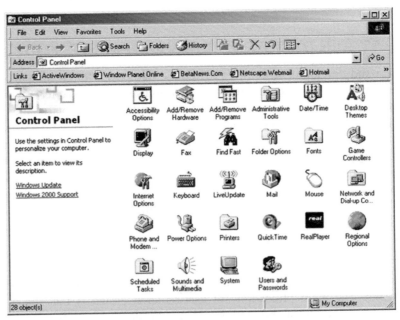

FIGURE 2.2 Microsoft Windows 2000 control panel—Feature-based design.

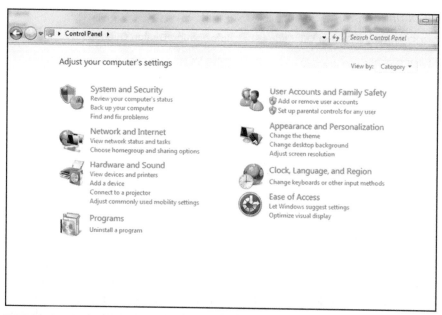

FIGURE 2.3 Microsoft Windows 7 control panel—task-based view.

Using a task-based approach and categorizing options make it easier for users to understand and navigate the system, providing a better overall experience. Regardless of the development model your team uses, it's a good idea to consider UCD when designing information and creating content. Before you begin defining the information and writing the text, asking yourself the following questions will help you get started:

UCD Software Design Questions	Information Design Question
Who is using this feature?	What are the characteristics of the people who will be using this feature? Is there one type of user or many users?
What is the user trying to do?	What is the user task? What is the user workflow? Is the task proactive or reactive? What does the user need to know before completing the task?
How is this need currently being met?	What tools is the user currently using? What terminology is currently used to describe the feature or options? What information is already available from other sources?
What is the user's level of ability?	What are the gaps between the user's current level of knowledge and the knowledge the user needs to use this feature?

Continued...

Continued	
UCD Software Design Questions	**Information Design Question**
What does the user need to complete this action?	What information does the user need to complete this task?
Does the proposed idea match the user expectations (wants and needs)	What information delivery mechanisms will best provide the information? What content types are best suited for each task?
How can we improve?	What information is missing or incomplete? How can we improve the information we already have? How can we better deliver the information?

DEVELOPMENT MODELS

Software development models provide the framework used to plan and execute software milestones and delivery cycles throughout the life of an application. While each design and development model has a different emphasis, they all follow the same basic flow of researching the requirements, design, implementation (coding), and verification or testing. The main difference is in the implementation of these phases. Most development models used today are variations of the classic waterfall model.

Waterfall Development Models

Waterfall development models follow a sequential design process. The benefit of this model is that since each phase only begins when another ends, the requirements and design of a program are finalized before any coding begins; this means that, resources, features, and program components are carefully planned and thought out before implementation begins.

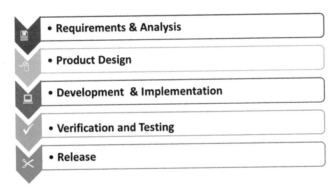

• Requirements & Analysis

• Product Design

• Development & Implementation

• Verification and Testing

• Release

FIGURE 2.4 Traditional waterfall model.

The disadvantage of the model is that when investing so much time in the early stages, any problems arising later on are often more difficult and expensive to revise. And the longer the cycles are, the greater the chance that requirements defined early in the process may no longer be relevant by the time the programmers actually begin coding. In a competitive market, time to market can mean the difference between a successful product and a product that is outdated before it is released. When this happens, teams often find themselves scrambling to revise and add features, creating a domino effect on the user interface text. As the development team revises the code, the text already designed and written generally becomes outdated as well, and you'll have to rethink and rewrite information that may have already been implemented and approved.

In response to these drawbacks, software development teams began switching over to an iterative or incremental approach to software development.

Iterative and Incremental Development Models

While the phases of an incremental design model are similar to those of the traditional waterfall model, iterative models use repeated cycles implemented in shorter increments of time. This allows the team to implement smaller changes throughout the development cycle.

In recent years, more teams have been using agile development, and it has become increasingly popular with both small and large organizations. This method uses iterative and incremental phases in which development tasks are broken into small increments completed over very short periods of time. Iterations follow the same basic steps as traditional development methods, but it's done on a feature-by-feature basis, with short cycles and releases available at the end of each cycle. This approach is considered agile in that it requires flexible management and development based on team collaboration and customer feedback. In an agile development environment, the foremost goal is to deliver the application quickly, and then add and update the application at regular intervals.

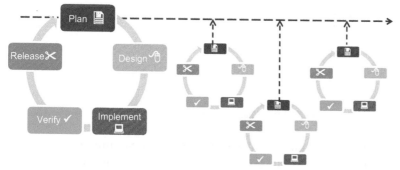

FIGURE 2.5 Example of an incremental model.

This incremental approach is particularly well suited for web applications where features can be updated on an ongoing basis, and users may not even be aware of subtle improvements and changes occurring from release to release. Frequent updates are considerably more difficult for packaged applications. However, at certain times, new features and updates can be downloaded from the product web site or from an executable file sent via e-mail.

Agile development has negative aspects as well. The first release of the application may be lacking in features, and users trying out the application in its initial phases may be disappointed by a lack of functionality and by poor performance. The text and guidance you build into the user interface will go a long way toward getting users excited about using the application. In addition, because the application is developed on a feature-by-feature basis, and often by different developers, it may lack cohesiveness. In an agile development setting, in order to provide a consistent experience, it's crucial that the user interface text and information experience be designed across all features.

ADDIE Instructional Design Model

The ADDIE instructional design model (Analysis, Design, Development, Implementation, Evaluation) is traditionally used by instructional designers and training specialists. This model, created in 1975, is still widely used to create and implement instructional training programs. Originally consisting of 19 separate steps, it was eventually pared down and grouped into five phases. At the time of its inception, the ADDIE model was entirely linear in its implementation (i.e., a waterfall model). However, later trends, such as iterative and incremental development and agile development frameworks, have influenced the implementation of the ADDIE model to include incremental, formative evaluation throughout the process.

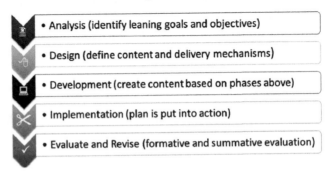

- Analysis (identify leaning goals and objectives)
- Design (define content and delivery mechanisms)
- Development (create content based on phases above)
- Implementation (plan is put into action)
- Evaluate and Revise (formative and summative evaluation)

FIGURE 2.6 Traditional ADDIE design model.

The main idea behind the ADDIE model is to determine the user's learning needs and then define the goals and objectives of a learning system based on those needs. This design model works well when thinking about the information users need, either within the user interface or delivered through another mechanism. Regardless of the development model your team uses, taking into account the ADDIE concept will help you think about the learning and instructional goals that will best meet the needs of your users.

DEVELOPMENT MODEL PHASES AND INFORMATION EXPERIENCE DESIGN

When designing and implementing the information experience, it's a good idea to follow the same model your team uses, mapping your activities to the relevant design phases and team schedules. This will keep your content aligned with the integration and delivery milestones of the application.

At each phase in the development cycle, you'll create your own goals and processes specific to the content and experience accompanying and integrated into each feature. The following diagram shows the types of activities the main roles will perform during different phases in the development cycle.[1]

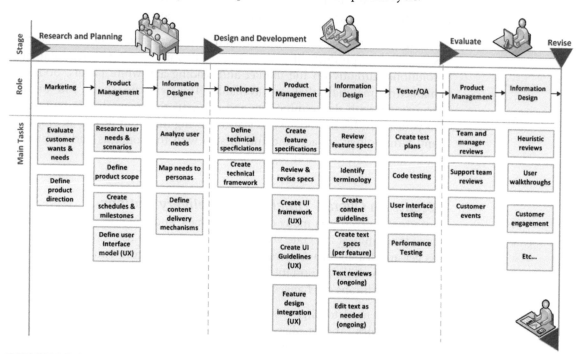

FIGURE 2.7 Summary of product phases and general tasks.

---

[1]Note that in this diagram, the UX role is included under product management as these two roles work in tandem with UX designers implementing the visual designs of the PM specifications.

Research and Planning (Analysis)

During the analysis phase, you are learning about your users so that you can identify the tasks they will need to complete and their learning needs for completing these tasks. Your product may have one, or many personas, and understanding the scenarios, tasks, knowledge levels, and motivation of your users is crucial for understanding the kind of information and type of interaction appropriate for your product and users.

Identifying the Learning Goals and Objectives

A good way to start understanding how users work with your application is by creating a list of all the tasks your users will perform and each step required for completing that task. Then next to each task, you should write down what information the user needs to complete the task, and what success looks like from the user's point of view. It's also a good idea to categorize tasks into phases, such as setting up, initial steps, configuring, monitoring, and maintenance, depending on the phases relevant for your users and their needs. This task analysis helps you identify and define user workflows and is the first step toward understanding the information workflow.

During the analysis phase, you should also learn about the technology or solution your product offers. You can do this my reading about competitor solutions currently on the market and reading any white papers, books, or marketing materials that are available. This will also help you become acquainted with the terminology and concepts that may already be familiar to your users. It's far too easy to start believing that your team's assumptions and terminology are accurate and in step with the concepts and terms your users are accustomed to using.

Create an Overall Timeline and Delivery Options

Information comes in many different formats, and you'll want to understand how you can best integrate your information into the user experience, as well as get an idea about what resources are available before you start designing. This is especially important if the delivery mechanisms for your content requires additions or changes to the program infrastructure and code.

You'll also need to align your content with the overall product milestones and schedules. At this phase, you should already start talking to the team about the methods and processes for getting your content reviewed and implemented. You'll also want to decide how you are going to give the content to the person responsible for coding the text. If you are entering the strings directly, it's tempting to skip the review stage: Having a process already established will help you keep all the important steps in place.

Once your team decides on the overall process, you can create your schedule, mapping each feature to the product development cycle and product milestones.

Design Phase and Development

During the design phase, you should start mapping user tasks and workflows to the proposed features and user experience. Mapping the tasks to user personas is a popular way to identify user needs and levels for interacting with each feature in the application. Details about creating personas are given in Section 2. Based on this mapping, you can determine the areas where users need instruction, guidance, and additional information.

During this phase, you'll also define the content delivery mechanisms and types, such as landing pages and help links, and create your guidelines for each content type. Let's say, for example, you decide that main pages in the application should have a help pane. In the design phase, you would create a general mock-up of a help pane, showing how the sections of the pane are divided, the structure for writing the links, and the hierarchy of how items are listed in the help pane. You will probably find it helpful to create templates for each content type as a framework for the actual text when you get to the development stage.

And it's generally a good idea to talk to the feature stakeholders about their main usability concerns for the tasks you've mapped out and for brainstorming different ideas, as well as for getting users over the learning curve. For example, if we go back to the example of the help pane, when you are specifying how help panes are designed, keep in mind that if you're not writing the help topics yourself, you'll also need to make sure that the person doing the writing has reviewed the design and is planning to provide the topics you've proposed.

Approaching the interface text as a feature and following design processes just as you would for any other feature will help you create a far better experience for your users.

Creating Your Processes

The design and development model a team uses ultimately influences its process for completing each product and each phase in the product cycle. Defining a process that works best for your team will help you stay on schedule and keep up with project milestones. It's important that the team accept your process and that you reevaluate your milestones and delivery points on a regular basis to ensure you're aligned with the product team schedules.

At the beginning stages, your process may begin as a simple flowchart, showing the main phases of your workflow for the overall design, each user task or per product feature. The example below shows a simple flow for how you may design and implement your content for each feature.

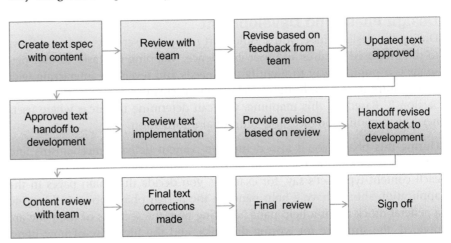

FIGURE 2.8 Sample process for content implementation.

Development Phase

The development phase begins when you start creating the actual content for integration into the application. While you're writing your text, you'll be working closely with your team's subject matter experts to ensure your content is accurate and provides the right level of information. Gathering as much feedback as possible on your proposed text is important to ensure you are providing the right information at the right time. This will help reduce the number of iterations later on, when it becomes more difficult to make changes. It's also a good idea to work with any other writers on the team who may be creating similar content for the documentation and online help.

You'll also want to think about tools and processes for presenting your designs and text to the team for review and implementation. If you have a designer, he or she may create a prototype. If you are working alone, you may find that Microsoft Office tools, such as Visio or PowerPoint, are useful for displaying your content as a workflow, using screen templates and actual screen captures.

Implementation Phase

When your content has been written and approved, it's ready to be implemented into the application. At this point, the text may be integrated into the spec that is handed off to the developer, or you may provide your own file with the approved text strings. In general, if you can provide strings that are copied and pasted into the code, you eliminate many chances for errors, such as spelling mistakes.

As your content is implemented, it's crucial that you review it within the context of the application. What feels right and reads well on paper may not read the same way when displayed within the user interface. It's also important to have your content reviewed by the feature stakeholders in particular and by anyone else who may be able to offer constructive feedback and insights, such as the technical writers and editors, and customer support engineers. If you are the main stakeholder (such as the product manager) or the developer, while you may know that the content is technically correct, you'll still want someone to review the usability of the text you have provided.

Evaluation and Revision

Regardless of how much effort goes into designing and developing your information and information experience, having it reviewed and tested is crucial. Whether the evaluation is informal, such as feature walkthroughs with the team or whether it is done using formal usability testing, the feedback enables you to improve your designs and content, thereby providing an optimal information experience. Instructions for how you can evaluate and test your content appears later in this book.

WORKING AS A TEAM

Up until now, this chapter talked about how design and development models are used to define and create applications. In this section we'll take a closer look at the roles and disciplines making up a typical team, and how the role of information designer interacts with the team throughout the process. Or course, each company structures its team according to its budget and needs: While large companies such as Microsoft and Google may have teams dedicated to each task, you may find yourself filling several roles in your organization. And while your team may not have someone designated with the specific titles described below, they are functions that someone on the team fills either formally or informally.

Team Tasks and Roles

Regardless of how clever, important, and useful your application is, a successful release is dependent on the team's ability to plan, collaborate, and work together. Even the most well-designed model or process depends on the talent of the team implementing it. And while each team is built somewhat differently, in general, most teams rely on these roles and tasks to create their applications.

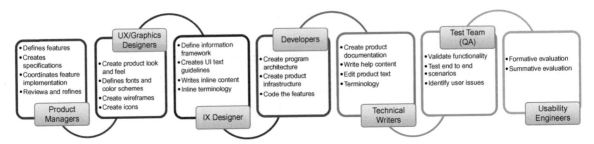

FIGURE 2.9 Example of main tasks and roles.

The role of information experience designer and his or her impact on the information experience and overall usability of an application have become increasingly important as user interfaces have become more interactive. The challenge of providing all the relevant information, without creating a text-heavy user interface involves careful planning and skillful crafting of your text. It also requires close cooperation between you and the other members of the team. Working together is paramount to the success of the information experience in particular and the project as a whole. And of course, with smaller teams in particular, you may find that you are performing several roles on the team.

Let's take a closer look at some of these roles, and their interaction and impact on the information experience throughout the process.

Information Experience Designer

The role of the information experience designer (IX design), as a professional, and within a team, is becoming increasingly common, particularly for web applications where very little, if any, supplemental reference materials are provided with an application. According to Edward Tufte, who is considered a world expert in visual design and information architecture, *information design* is the presentation of design to facilitate understanding, and *information architecture* is the structural design of information in space to facilitate intuitive access to content. Information experience designers often have the challenge of combining both of these skills into one role—not only defining the content, but also deciding which delivery mechanisms and navigation models are appropriate and best suited for the application and specific user tasks.

Working with the product manager and user experience designer (if you are lucky to have one) will help you create a clearly defined set of goals for your content, based on real use-cases, user tasks, and user workflows and on the product navigation model. As you create the information goals, you'll need to consider the skill levels of your users, the complexity of the application, and the environment, or platform, in which your end users will interact with the application.

As the next example shows, defining the information experience and architecture requires a different approach depending on whether your application is running on a desktop or a mobile device. Many applications are optimized to run on both.

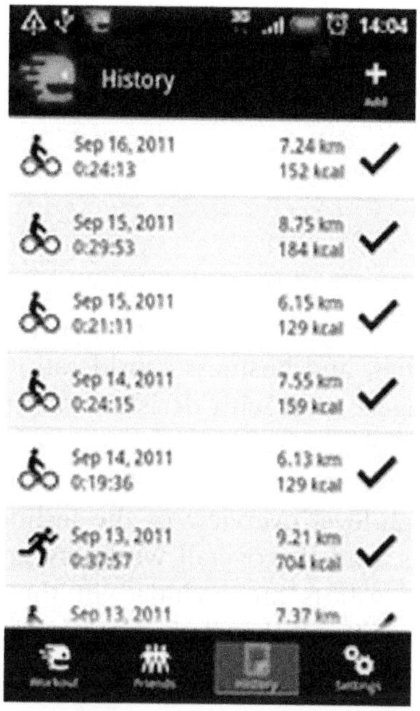

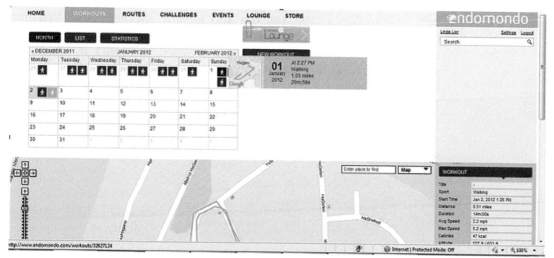

FIGURE 2.10 Exercise workout history on a mobile device (Endomondo).

FIGURE 2.11 Exercise workout history on a desktop computer (Endomondo).

After the information experience model is complete, you may be crafting the text yourself, or you may be working with a technical writer to create and edit the text strings. In addition, you'll probably need to work closely with the software developers to verify that the text messages within the user interface follow your text guidelines and provide the right information. Whether you come from a programming, product manager, technical writing, or any other background, your goal and process remains the same—to provide users with the information they need at the time they need it.

Project Manager

Project managers (also called product managers) are responsible for defining the new features and components of an application or system based on user needs, system capabilities, and business considerations. To gather this information, product managers meet with decision makers, the marketing team, and end users to determine which features are included in an application and the specifications for implementing those features. The specifications generally include a high-level overview of the technology, a description of the need and use-cases, and the overall workflow and end-user experience. Generally, sample screenshots are included in the specifications. Product managers work closely with all the disciplines and have a lot of input into the interaction design and user interface text.

By working with the product manager as the feature evolves, you can begin learning about the user workflows and tasks early on in the design phase, identifying areas where users may need specific information or help to complete a task. You can also identify any new terms that may need clarification. The earlier in the process you get started understanding the information needs and defining a glossary, the easier it will be for you to understand and define the scope of work required. Feature specs usually go through a review process with the team creating the feature. This example shows a typical spec review process: As you can see from the process, the information and user experience designers are involved early on in the process, collaborating with each other and with the product manager.

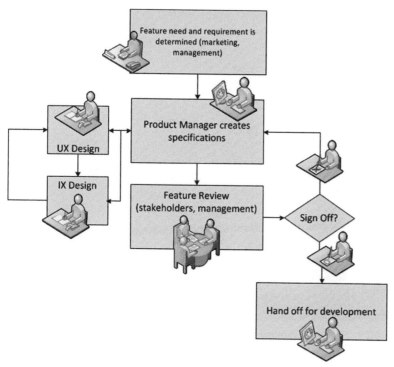

FIGURE 2.12 Example of a feature spec review process.

Working with the product managers during the planning stage is an ideal time for the information designer to define the points within an application workflow where users will most benefit from instruction and information.

User Experience Designer

User experience (UX) designers understand how users interact with applications, and how graphics and design are integrated to create the user interface and interaction models. The UX designer creates mockups (wireframes) of the surfaces comprising the product and works closely with the product manager to create the overall look and feel of each feature. Wireframes may be interactive, providing not only the layout and visual representation of the screens, but also showing the interaction between screens, the workflow, and the navigation model.

By working closely with the UX designer from the very beginning, you can start defining how your content is presented and embedded within the context of the user experience. You can also start creating text guidelines, providing sample user interface text, defining the types of help links that will be included, and starting to define the nomenclature that will be used throughout the application.

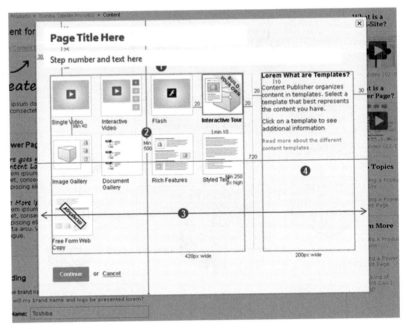

FIGURE 2.13 Sample wireframe.

And this is how the page looks after the design and text are complete.

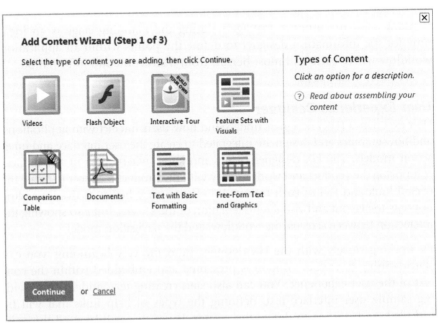

FIGURE 2.14 The page with text and help links.

While some organizations may have distinct roles for the user experience designer and interaction designer, often these roles are combined, with one person creating both the design and interaction model. On smaller teams, each product manager may have to take on the role of user experience designer for their features and for the product as a whole.

Graphic Designer

Depending on the application, a graphic designer may be called in to add the visual components to the application. Some applications, such as games and educational programs, which have a strong graphical presence, are more likely to include a graphic artist or designer as part of the team. Where the user experience designer creates the overall framework, interactive model, and layouts, the graphic designer defines visual elements and colors, specifying how buttons, labels, banners, icons and fonts, and any graphical elements appear in the screens. On many teams, the user experience designer is also responsible for graphics and visuals.

When designing your information, it's also important for you to pay attention to the impact of colors and fonts on the overall information experience. Overusing colors and fonts to call attention to text can result in pages that are too busy, lacking flow and focus. If you don't have UX or graphic designers working with you, it's best to keep things very simple, using any boldface and colored fonts sparingly and consistently.

Software Developers

Although careful planning, feature specs, and design are important to the success of any application, it's the software developers who create the code that gets the application running. Prior to programming a feature, the software developer is often required to write a development spec, defining the programming structure and architecture of that feature.

While developers have a deep understanding of how an application works, they generally have very little, if any, contact with actual users. Therefore, they often don't understand the end-user skills and capabilities, the common usage scenarios, and user workflows. During the coding process, it's important for the person responsible for writing the text to work with the developer, providing the user interface content and looking for areas in which information is missing and required.

Developers often create messages, such as errors and validation messages, while they are in the midst of programming a feature. The messages developers write are often cryptic and technical, and if they go unnoticed, they often become part of the released product. Even when the developer is a talented writer, a writer should review all messages within the user interface, even validation messages.

FIGURE 2.15 Example of a programmer error message.

FIGURE 2.16 Example of a helpful error message.

Technical Writers

Even before developers start coding, the technical writers are planning the documentation deliverables, milestones, and schedules. While documentation is generally developed alongside an application as reference material, many technical writers are also finding themselves moving into the role of information experience design, preparing and editing the text that appears within the user interface of the application. If you are finding yourself moving into the role of information experience design, the skills you already use in defining and designing documentation and help content will be of value when you are designing and writing the content appearing in the user interface.

While writing the documentation, the technical writer is often the first person to walk through a given feature from start to finish. This provides many opportunities for providing usability input and suggesting ways to improve the flow of content and the text within the user interface.

As the information experience designer, you and the technical writers should work together to decide on terminology and on the interaction and integration between the text in the user interface and the online help. Documentation can be provided in a variety of mediums, and working closely as a team will help you define the content types and delivery methods that are best suited for the information your users need.

USER DOCUMENTATION AND USER INTERFACE TEXT

David Farbey

London UK, Professional Technical Communicator, ISTC Council Member, and Chair of the Technical Communication UK 2012 Conference, http://www.farbey.co.uk

Many software companies still operate with strict demarcation between the work of software engineers, user experience designers, and technical writers, but in my experience it's always beneficial when these three roles work collaboratively.

Of these three professions, the technical writer is often the closest to the true end users. Technical writers make an effort to understand end users' jobs, so that they can provide instructions for using the software or the app to do those jobs. The job may involve anything from processing accounts to designing circuit boards, and people would need to do those jobs whether or not they had this particular software product at their disposal. Good user instructions should focus on real-world tasks, not software steps.

This user task focus can help improve the design of products and make sure that elements are presented in a way that's logical for users. The way the software actually works can remain safely hidden away. Even where it's not possible to improve the product design, often a very brief on-screen text or popup suggested by the team's technical writer can remind users of what to do at a particular moment, so they won't need to interrupt the flow of their work to find information in online help.

For years people in the software industry have been dreaming of applications that are so easy to use—so "intuitive"—that user instructions of any kind would be unnecessary. Today we have thousands of apps for tablets and smartphones that "just work" and for which there is nothing we would recognize as online help. However, a smartphone app is designed to do just one thing—for example, get the weather forecast for a given location. In contrast, business software and personal productivity suites (word processors and spreadsheets, for example) remain complicated. The need for good instructions will remain for a long time to come.

Testing Team (QA)

Software development teams have quality-assurance testers who are responsible for reviewing each feature separately and the application as a whole. Software testers are checking the software for performance issues and code bugs for the various user scenarios. At the same time, the QA team also checks for problems affecting the user experience, which includes incomplete or inaccurate text, broken help links, and typographical errors and inconsistencies. The test team can be a valuable resource for the information experience designer as they encounter the messages and user interface text within the context of user actions for a wide range of use-cases and scenarios.

Although the testers are reviewing the software, they can check that the messages within the interface make sense, are in the right location, and provide the right information. They can also check that validation messages and error messages are provided as needed and that the messages are helpful and accurate. Providing your test team with a checklist of what they should look for is useful for them to help find areas that should be fixed or improved.

Usability Engineers

Usability engineers are responsible for validating that the designs and interaction models meet user expectations and provide the right user experience. Usability engineers use a variety of methods and tools, such as heuristic evaluations, card sorting, usability tests, and focus groups, to understand how users interact with your application, to find what makes sense to users, and to pinpoint the areas of confusion. Based on their research, usability engineers provide recommendations for improving designs based on their research. Your team may or may not have a usability engineer as part of the team, or may be called in as consultants at various milestones during a project. If your team doesn't have access to a usability professional, you can use a number of methods to gather feedback about the text you've provided and the overall information experience. Methods for validating and evaluating the information experience are described later on in this book.

USING A TEAM DECISION MATRIX

Because so many of the design tasks overlap, sometimes it's difficult to tell where one role ends and another begins. And while an overlapping of skills and roles can ultimately lead to a better end result, it can also cause confusion as to who leads the various efforts, who "owns" what, and who makes the final decisions. And when it comes to what's written in the user interface, there are always many different opinions as to what users need and how it should be presented.

Many teams rely on a decision-making matrix to clarify who owns the decisions and who are the participants. One common model is called OARP (Owner, Accountable, Reviewer, Participant).

FIGURE 2.17 The OARP decision-making model.

- Owner: Provides sign-off on the feature, including the design and text
- Accountable: Is directly responsible but does not have the final decision-making authority
- Reviewer: Has expertise and provides recommendations
- Participant: Provides data for decision making

In the OARP model, the final decision maker is clearly defined as the approver. If the reviewer and owner are not in agreement, they may escalate to a manager or to whoever has the final decision-making power.

Having a decision-making model in place helps teams move forward when they experience problems agreeing on ideas or designs. If your team has a decision-making matrix, make sure you are aware of it, and that you understand who the final approver is of your designs and content.

SUMMARY

In this chapter, you learned about different approaches for creating an application and about different design models, together with the roles within the team. In his book, *The Inmates Are Running the Asylum*, Alan Cooper suggests that software projects fail when they try to be all things to all people. Keeping focused on the user and on the tasks your users are trying to accomplish, while working within the boundaries of your team's schedules and resources, is key to defining a process that works best for designing and delivering your information.

- Design and development models go hand in hand, and provide the processes for creating systems that meet user needs and that provide a positive end-user experience.
- User-centered design models focus on user needs, abilities, and tasks.

- Waterfall development models are sequential, with one phase completing before another phase begins. The benefit of this model is that the requirements at each step are met before moving on to the next stage in the process, according to well-defined guidelines.
- Iterative development models evaluate and improve designs throughout the product development cycle.
- Incremental design models release a version of the product, and then add and improve features on an ongoing basis. This model is particularly well suited for web applications.
- A successful release is dependent on the team's ability to plan, collaborate, and work together. For this purpose, team schedules and tasks should be well defined.
- A decision-making matrix is useful when there are conflicting ideas.

Understanding User Needs

After your team has decided on their development process and schedule, the next step in designing your information is understanding the needs, expectations, and goals of the intended users. This step requires planning and research, but the payoff will be well worth the effort as the data you gather will help you understand the scope and depth of the information your users will need. Without gathering this information, you may end up relying on the assumptions made by other members of the team—who may have never even met a real user. Trying to think like a user, without empirical observations or input, can lead you down the wrong path, where your content and information may be too complicated, overly simplistic, or irrelevant to your users' actual tasks and goals.

This section describes general types of user groups, the types of tasks different users have, and how you can create personas to help you understand the needs of your users.

CHAPTER 3

Getting to Know Your Users

INTRODUCTION

The importance of understanding the target audience for your application isn't newly recognized; actually, marketing research firms spend countless hours running focus groups, surveying, and interviewing people to understand potential markets and users for their clients' products. When it comes to designing software applications, and the content within them, the same diligence should be applied for understanding the needs, knowledge levels, and working environment of potential users. Large corporations often have entire teams dedicated to user research or pay large amounts of money for someone to do it for them. Although your company may not be able to devote the same amount of time and manpower as some corporations and companies, without investing some time in understanding who your users are, and what they do, it will be difficult to create the information that meets their needs.

UNDERSTANDING YOUR USERS

One method frequently used to understand and keep focused on the user is to create user personas. A persona is a fictitious character representing a key user group for your product. Your application may have several personas, each based on the specific characteristics and attributes of a major user group for your application.

When creating the content for your application, personas can help you to understand how your users search for information, their information needs, and their current levels of knowledge. This will help you use terminology and create text and guidelines that will match user needs and expectations and filling the knowledge gaps. It will also help you create button labels and links that users are inclined to click.

You can use common user research methodologies to gather your data on personas and learn about the people who will be using your application; later in this section, you'll read about these different methodologies. The data you'll need to build your personas depends on the type and complexity of the application. For example, the relevant characteristics of business users, such as network administrators, will differ significantly from those of users of entertainment applications (such as media downloads and online shopping), or users of productivity applications (e.g., home accounting, travel booking)—even though, in actuality, the same person may, at one time or another, use all three, and additional types of applications.

This chapter looks at different types of applications and the kinds of users who rely on the information you provide when interacting with these applications.

IDENTIFYING YOUR USER TYPES

Applications are often described as falling either into the **business** or the **consumer** category. Business applications, as the name implies, are used within companies (e.g., banks, corporate offices, airports) and organizations such as educational systems, government offices, and medical institutions to facilitate business goals. Consumer applications are meant for personal or home use and may be downloaded, used online, or purchased from a retailer.

It's easy to get carried away and to identify every person and user who may come in contact with the application as a persona. Creating too many personas may have an adverse effect: Instead of helping you focus on real user needs and abilities, you may find yourself creating text and information that explains too much to some users and not enough to others. To avoid this pitfall, when thinking about your personas, you should also categorize them according to priority, as follows:

> **Primary users**—the main users of the application. These are the personas you should focus on when you are developing your information experience. For example, in a networking application, this would be the network administrator responsible for configuring and monitoring the application. If, for example, you are creating an application for online banking, your primary persona would be the bank customer, who wants to view statements, pay bills, and purchase stocks.
> **Secondary users**—users who may interact with the application but are not included in the primary user group. You may consider these users

but won't base your designs on their needs. For example, in the networking example, this may be the administrator who is responsible for setting up user permissions for the application, or who needs to make some adjustments to the system but is not responsible for the overall configuration. In the online banking scenario, this may be the person looking for information about bank services and offers, but not necessarily a bank customer.

Insignificant users—users who may interact with the application but are not part of the primary or secondary user groups. These are users who use the product occasionally or in unintended ways. You don't need to consider these users when designing your information. However, it is important to know about this group so that you don't miss any opportunities for bringing them into the other groups or so that you don't inadvertently bring them to the forefront of your designs.

Aside from these three groups, you may need to consider the needs of other groups of stakeholders, although they may not be associated with a specific target persona:

- **Important customers:** If your most important customer doesn't match your primary users, you may still need to consider their needs when making decisions. In most cases, there will probably be overlap with your primary users, but in some instances you may need to make adjustments based on the needs of specific users or a specific group of users.
- **Stakeholders, such as resellers and business partners:** You may need to consider the requests and needs of these users, in particular when your application is marketed as part of a bundle or another product. Also, keep in mind that resellers and business partners may be more aware of market trends and user needs. Considering their requests and then validating them with your own research may help you understand your users' needs.

BUSINESS APPLICATIONS AND THEIR USERS

Business applications are purchased to provide services or a solution to a business need—helping a business grow, improving productivity, or managing an aspect of the business. Business applications include shared calendars, intranet sites, accounting programs, inventory databases, e-mail services, as well as common word processing and project management applications. Because business applications cover a wide range of uses with different levels of experience and needs, there may be more than one type of primary and secondary users and target user groups for any given application.

For example, an online accounting application may have to meet the needs of several users:

- **Employees** use the tool to request a budget for purchases or reimbursement for travel expenses.
- **Managers** use the tool to approve employee requests and track team budgets and spending.
- **Administrative staff** tracks outgoing purchase orders and payments from the accounting office.

Each of these users requires a different set of options and instructions. Let's see how many people are involved in the purchasing and implementation of a simple business application.

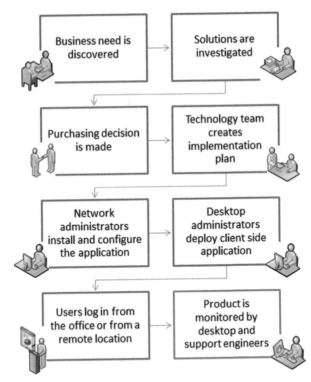

In the accompanying diagram, you can see that while many steps may be involved in the purchasing and planning of an application, at the point of implementation, the number of actual users is much smaller. In this example, there are four actual users or user groups:

- Network administrators who install and configure the application
- Desktop administrators, clients who log into the application

- Desktop and support who monitor the application
- End users who may not even be aware they are using the application

The business decision makers and planning team, while interested in how the application can be used to meet the business needs, may never actually work with the application itself.

Network Administrators

Network administrators (also referred to as IT administrators) are responsible for installing, implementing, and maintaining business applications for an organization or company. Often these applications require intricate infrastructure and server configurations. Network administrators have varying levels of skills and expertise. Depending on your application, you'll need to determine the information your users need and the best ways to present it to the network administrators responsible for installing and configuring your application. You may find that there are several network administrator personas for a single product, for example:

- Server administrator responsible for setting up the network infrastructure required to install and deploy the application
- Network administrator responsible for installing and configuring the application
- Network administrator responsible for monitoring and maintenance
- Desktop administrator responsible for deploying the application on client computers and for ongoing support of the client-side application

Because network administrators and their colleagues are responsible for keeping the network running smoothly, they need to understand what the feature does, and its impact on the entire network.

> "Network administrators want under-the-hood information. They want to understand how a feature works, not just what it does."
> **—Gershon Levitz, Senior Technical Writer at Microsoft**

Client-Side Business Users

After a business application is up and running, it may be completely transparent to the user (as in the case of a network monitoring application, or firewall), or it may provide a tool that can be used in the office, or accessed from a remote computer or hand-held device (e.g., expense and purchasing tool, document repository, conferencing tool).

Although the skills and knowledge levels of the network administrators tend to have some consistencies, client-side users come from any number of backgrounds, educational levels, skill levels, and personalities. These tools are becoming increasingly sophisticated. While everything was once done locally or on a network server, desktop users now need to understand how to access and save and interact with an application from any number of places, such as the cloud, and all their devices (desktop, laptop, smart phone, tablet, etc.).

In addition to personal differences, the same application may have entirely different, yet equally important, user groups. For example, an application used to schedule and manage medical appointments may be used by a number of users: patients, administration staff, and doctors.

Patient	Administrator	Doctor
• Search for doctors • Schedule or change appointments • Find test results	• Confirm and schedule appointments • Block out dates • Tracks working hours and statistics	• Set up office hours • Print appointment list • Track patient hours • Update patient data

Each of these is a primary user, with a different set of needs and varying levels of computer literacy, both across groups and within groups.

Examples of client-side target users include the following:

- Clients sharing information in a central repository—where each user has a client component installed on his or her workstation, but the information is uploaded and stored in a central location (database). These clients may be allowed to access the repository from a desktop or remote computer (laptop, tablet, hand-held devices).
- Software as a service (SaaS) clients—where the application is hosted in the "cloud" and users log into the application using a web browser.
- Users of business software programs—where each user has a licensed version of a business application installed on their workstation. Business applications range from common word processing programs, such as Office Word, and presentation software to computer software, such as AutoCAD used by architects for designing and drafting.
- Client component is installed on each computer, providing a network service, such as Active Directory or Remote Desktop Connection. Although these users are important, they are secondary users, since their role requires little interaction with the application. And while the interaction between the client and the application must be positive, the main user of this application is the administrator responsible for configuring and maintaining the functionality.

When designing information for client-side users, remember that as opposed to network administrators, they aren't interested in how the application works. They may need simple troubleshooting information, but mainly, they only need enough information to keep the application running smoothly.

CONSUMER APPLICATIONS AND THEIR USERS

Consumer applications are used by individuals for personal use. These applications may provide a service, such as home accounting or cloud storage services, or they may be used for entertainment purposes (e.g., music downloads, games, online photo albums).

Although consumer software applications were at one time packaged by the manufacturer and purchased from a retailer, consumer applications include web applications, shareware, and apps that are either used online or downloaded onto a computer or mobile device. Along with understanding the application, these users must also navigate through the download and purchasing process without any printed materials to guide them. All the information must be built into the application. Purchasing and delivering consumer products can be done in different ways, depending on the application and market.

When compared to the model for how business applications are purchased and installed, the consumer model relies only on the user and their abilities to decide which application to use and to figure out how to use it. If the process is easy and intuitive, users will be happy and continue using the application; if the process is frustrating and difficult, users will choose a different application.

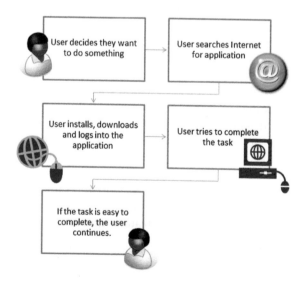

Defining user groups and personas for a consumer application is somewhat more difficult than defining business users. Each application may have several groups of users, and each group may include different backgrounds and age groups. Before you create personas, you can start thinking about the kinds of users who will be interested in purchasing or using your application and their information needs.

One way of categorizing consumer users is according to their computer proficiency levels. This is not the same as creating personas, but it will help you remember that you are writing for a variety of users, with varying levels of skills. It will also help you think about the kind of information your users will need.

- **Novice users**—While it's getting more difficult to find novice users, there are still people who are just getting around to jumping on the computer bandwagon. Novice users have a few tasks they complete with an application, interacting with only a few of the available options and features to complete the most common tasks. Novice users need a lot of support when they do decide to venture beyond their comfort zone. If novice users are occasional users, it will take more prodding and pushing to get them to try new tasks. If they use an application on a regular basis, at some point they should be ready to try new tasks. Keep in mind that providing support is different than providing a lot of text. Too much text or technical information can be overwhelming. These users need to know exactly what to do to start and complete a task and what to expect along the way. Also, remember that someone who is considered a novice for one type of application may be more proficient in another type of application, such as computer games.
- **Beginners**—While these users may already be comfortable using the applications and features they are familiar with, they still only use the application in a distinct number of tasks, and in limited ways, trying out other features only when the need arises. These users probably want to increase their knowledge and improve their skills—learning how to do things more efficiently or trying new tasks if they know what's available and how to get started. These users want to know how to complete tasks more efficiently and how to increase the value they are getting from an application.
- **Experienced users**—These are the users who are comfortable with most applications, even if they are somewhat unfamiliar with the technology. These users will look for advanced features and settings if they will help

them use the application and complete tasks more efficiently. These users will read some of the user interface text, if it looks important and is easily noticeable.

- **Super users**—These are the early adopters, computer geeks, and computer professionals who are very comfortable configuring applications. These are the users who look for advanced options and who like to get in under the hood to see how things work. They also customize the application. When writing interactive content, you don't need to worry too much about these users: They like to figure it out on their own. What these users do need, however, are good warnings and error messages, which help them understand what not to do and to troubleshoot when issues arise.

Thinking about the user categories even before you delve deeper into the personas for your application helps you build text into your application that is relevant for the proficiency levels of different users. It also helps you keep in mind how user levels impact their interaction with the application.

Off-the-Shelf Applications

Since off-the-shelf applications are purchased through a retailer, users have generally made a purchasing decision and have decided to use the application. This means that their motivation to succeed is high, but that they also expect the application to be easy to understand and use.

Since technology is now a part of our everyday lives, users who have no technical knowledge are purchasing hardware and software products to install on their home computers. Users who purchase these applications often find themselves trying to complete tasks that are beyond their comfort level and skills—setting up home routers, modems, audio systems, and private home networks. These products often require users to change their computer settings and manipulate wires, which are completely unfamiliar to them. Finding the right level of information for home users is not a trivial endeavor.

For the novice and beginning users, the information you provide needs to instill confidence and guide them, providing the right level of details and troubleshooting advice. In the example below, the writers put the users at ease by letting them know exactly what they will be doing and by emphasizing that the wizard will guide them through each step. More experienced users will only read as much information as they need, but will benefit from the explanations and instructions provided for less savvy users.

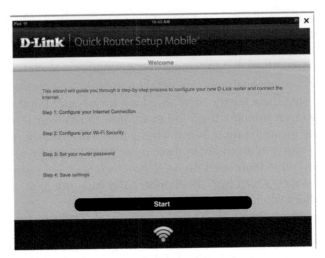

FIGURE 3.1 QRS Mobile application on the iPad.

Home entertainment and media software, such as computer games and video editors, require less information and have little margin of failure, but these users have high expectations—that the products will be quick and easy to set up and run.

One challenge presented in writing user interface text for packaged applications is deciding what level of information to include in the interface and what information can be placed elsewhere. In a home networking product, users are generally working at a slower pace and will look at the help when they are stuck, or want to learn more about the application. In an entertainment application, such as a game or photo editor, users are intent on what they are doing at the time, and the user interface is often only a source of information users are willing to read.

FIGURE 3.2 Example of a game application (Microsoft Age of Empires).

When you think about who is going to purchase and install your application, think about what happens when the users get the application home. What's the first piece of information they'll need when they open the package and insert the disk into the disk drive, and what's the first action they will need to take? Think about a few possible users of different age groups and their levels of confidence and knowledge. This will provide a baseline for understanding the minimum amount of information and the type of instructions these users will need throughout the process.

Downloadable Tools and Applications

Every year an increasing number of applications and tools are available by downloading them directly from the Internet. These applications may be provided free of charge, for a monthly fee, or for purchase. Depending on your application, your users may represent a variety of ages, backgrounds, and educational levels. Regardless of their demographics, users are somewhat reluctant to download applications and often want to use them for a trial period before making a purchase. Free applications may not need a trial period, but users may not use them after downloading them if they are not easy to install and figure out.

All the information for downloading and getting started with such an application should be readily available within the download pages and main pages of the application. Getting users through the download process with guidance and support and letting them know what to expect when they click the download or install link will positively impact the likelihood of their using your application.

In the following examples, users can clearly understand what is being installed with each component and the changes that will be made to their computers.

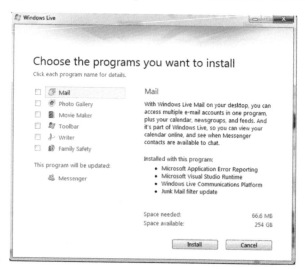

FIGURE 3.3 Example of a download page (Microsoft Windows Live).

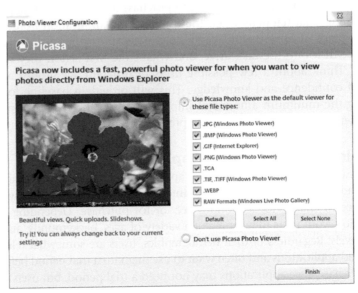

FIGURE 3.4 Example of download settings (from Picasa).

While an online help file is generally provided as part of the download, most users rely strictly on the text within the user interface to guide them and get them started using the application. In the application below, which was downloaded from the Internet, the options are clearly labeled, and each element on the screen is explained using tooltips. While an online help system is provided, users have enough information available within the user interface to perform common tasks.

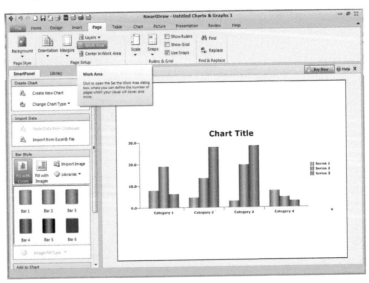

FIGURE 3.5 Smartdraw application screen (downloaded from Smartdraw.com).

When you think about users for a downloadable application, and the kind of information they need, think about your main tasks and then imagine the kind of user who may need or want to complete those tasks. For example, in the graphics program above, you may start by thinking about a student completing a report, a small-business owner creating a business presentation, and a teacher creating a lesson.

Web Tools and Applications

With web tools and applications, users can create an account, log in, and use the application or tool that is hosted on a web site. Web applications range from business and productivity tools to entertainment applications and online, interactive games. Because users don't need to download the application, they are more willing to try them out and play around with the settings before deciding to actually use the application.

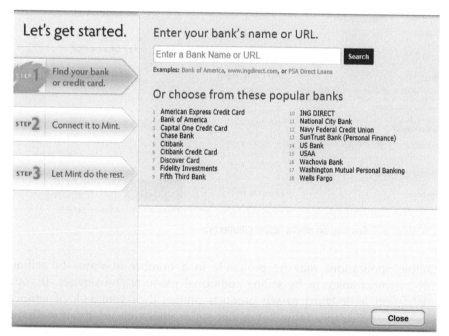

FIGURE 3.6 Example of an online home productivity application (Mint.com).

Most of the information needed to use and interact with the application is embedded into the user interface and is provided online. In these tools, the layout of your information helps users understand the workflow and is as crucial as the text itself.

Online applications provided for productivity, such as online accounting, are obviously geared toward a different type of user mind-set than online games and entertainment sites. The information you provide should be geared toward the mind-set of the users when they are sitting in front of your application, completing common tasks.

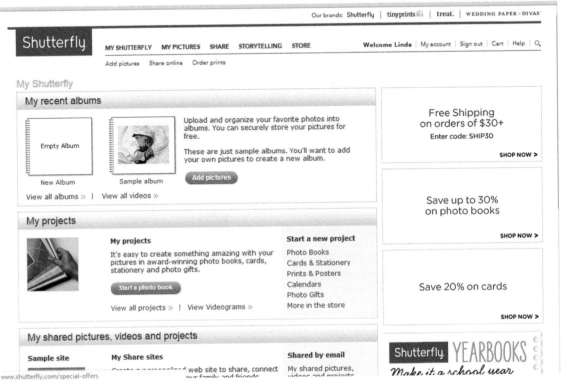

FIGURE 3.7 Creating an album online (Shutterfly).

Online applications may be profitable in a number of ways—by selling advertisement space or by selling additional products and services. If your application is designed to sell products online, then your task of writing information becomes more complicated—incorporating information about additional products into the page without interfering with the user experience.

Mobile Apps
Countless mobile applications are available for smartphone operating systems (e.g., iPhone, Android, BlackBerry, and Windows Phone). These apps are available directly from the phone and include anything from tools to

online games to simple widgets that are downloaded directly onto the phone.

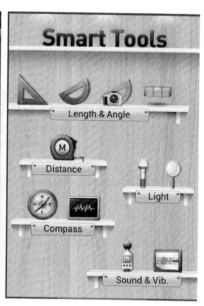

FIGURE 3.8 Example of apps for mobile phones.

While the mode of interaction is different, writing for mobile apps is not much different from web applications. There are additional considerations, such as the interaction method, and therefore terminology is different. For example, in a mobile app, users tap, not click, and they slide instead of drag. And, of course, the size of the user interface limits the amount of text and string length. But keeping the user in mind and understanding the user's information needs are still the main concerns of writing for mobile apps.

From a user perspective, now that mobile devices have become mainstream, with people of all ages and backgrounds purchasing them, it's hard to pinpoint a typical user of many applications and widgets. It's helpful to think about different age groups when planning text for mobile apps, and to build your text around the group who will likely need the most assistance from your primary users. For mobile apps, teenagers who grew up keeping their Tamaguchi pets alive and playing video games are more likely to fall into the experienced and super-user categories, while older users, with less experience, need more instructions and guidance. In the examples above, it's quite possible that users in every category range from late childhood to late adulthood.

SUMMARY

Learning about your users and how they will use your application is one of the first steps toward designing and creating your information experience. Each type of application, business and consumer, has primary and secondary users you should consider when planning your information experience strategy.

- Business applications are used within companies and organizations to facilitate business goals.
- Consumer applications are meant for personal or home use.
- Understanding the needs of your users is critical for designing information that meets those needs.
- Business users generally consist of server and network administrators responsible for configuring and deploying an application, desktop administrators responsible for making sure the application runs on the client computers and devices, and client-side users.
- Consumer users come from a variety of backgrounds and levels, but generally consist of novice, beginner, experienced, and super users.

CHAPTER 4

Gathering Data about Your Users

INTRODUCTION

Learning about your users and understanding how they use your application are important for ensuring that the content you create meets their information needs. Simple research methodologies can be used to learn about your users, their work practices, and what motivates them to use your application. This can be a daunting task, and it's easy to become overwhelmed with facts and data. Creating a plan and limiting your research to common user tasks and goals will help you stay focused. A good way to start is by thinking about user goals, as well as the tasks your users will want to complete to meet those goals. Then define your research plan and questions around those goals. After gathering your data, you'll analyze it, looking for similarities among groups. Finally, you'll use the data to understand your target users and create personas.

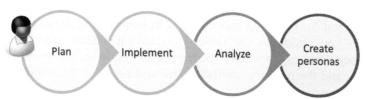

The amount of time you spend gathering data is essentially determined by the amount of time and resources available. Regardless of time constraints, certain basic steps are involved in gathering data that can help you understand your users and that can be used for creating personas later on.

- **Plan**—During this stage you define and create your research tools. You decide what research methodologies you will use and how you will implement them. You will also need to find people who may represent your target user groups from whom you will collect data, and you will decide the number of people you will use in your research.

- **Implement**—During this stage, you gather demographic and other qualitative information you will use to learn about your target users. And while you may be working toward building personas as a team effort, remember that you need to gather data about your users' information needs and habits.
- **Analyze**—After collecting the information, you will need to aggregate your data, mapping your findings to real user tasks and goals. Remember that you are looking for trends and data about how your users interact with the user interface and how they use the information and text provided in the user interface (e.g., explanatory text, links).
- **Create personas**—Based on your research, you can create personas, each representing a target user group. And while you may have any number of user types and potential personas, narrowing them down to a few personas who exemplify your target users will be the basis of your persona biographies.

GATHERING THE USER DATA

Gathering data to create personas is a good way to learn about the everyday working practices, knowledge levels, and information needs of your users. You can use common user research methodologies to gather your data; these methods include surveys, customer interviews, site visits, and focus groups. As your application begins to develop, usability studies and user walk-throughs of the initial designs will help you further refine your data. In addition, any information gathered from the marketing group or other user-facing members of the team is useful—as long as you are able to distinguish between fact and opinion.

Each method for gathering user data has its benefits and drawbacks, and the methods you decide to use depend on having realistic plans and goals. Before beginning any research, you'll need to decide on the amount of time you have and the resources available. This will help you determine the scope of your research.

CREATING USER SURVEYS

A survey is a data collection tool used to gather information about individuals and groups. Because user surveys often rely on close-ended questions and can be administered electronically, they are a good tool for gathering information that can easily be evaluated and analyzed. Because surveys let you gather relatively large amounts of statistical data in a relatively short period of time, they are particularly useful for gathering information from a large number of people.

Surveys are a reliable method for gathering factual data about your users, such as age ranges, educational levels, and facts about their working environment. Gathering other types of information, such as user opinions, likes and dislikes, and trends in user behavior, is more difficult but can be done with careful planning. When creating your survey questions, consider the goal of each question, asking yourself what you are trying to measure. Then you need to decide on the best format for that question and the participant selection options. All these issues will influence the type of information you gather from the survey.

Building Your Survey Questions

Surveys may focus on gathering factual information and may be used to learn the opinions of the survey takers. While it's easier to build questions for factual information, there are several ways you can build your survey questions to gather subjective information, such as using rating scales and multiple choice. Each provides a slightly different level of data. You can see an example of this in the samples below. Let's say, for example, you want to know if your users prefer to access information in the user interface by having text displayed inline, directly on the page, or by clicking help links to open explanations and descriptions. The type of question you provide and the choices that are available will influence the data. The following examples show how subtle changes in format can affect your data.

   Rating scales: One way to measure user likes and dislikes and user attitudes is to use rating scales. With rating scales, participants are given a statement, and then they select their level of agreement with the statement.

User Survey Sample – Rating Scales					
	Strongly disagree	Disagree	No opinion	Agree	Strongly Agree
Help links area a good way to provide information.	○	○	○	○	○
The last time I clicked a help link the information was what I needed.	○	○	○	○	○
If a help link is available, I am likely to click on it.	○	○	○	○	○

Typically, a rating scale (also called Likert scales) will have one to five or one to seven choices, with a neutral choice provided.

Paired comparison: Paired comparison questions present two statements, and the participants choose which statement they agree with or prefer. Paired questions have the benefit of providing two distinct options, and the users are forced to select the one that best describes their feelings or actions. Based on the answers, you can conclude that one option or scenario is preferable to the other.

User Survey Sample – Paired Comparison

What statement best describes you?

○ I like help links because they give me the information only when I need it.
That way I don't have extra information on the screen.

○ I don't like help links because clicking the link requires an extra step. I'd rather
have the information on the page where it's visible.

Because neither selection in the pair may actually describe the participants' feelings or actions, you may also want to include a space for comments in case participants want to qualify their answer.

Multiple choice: Multiple-choice questions let participants chose their answer from among several possibilities. These may be Yes/No questions, or you may provide a list of possibilities and allow participants to choose one or more options from the list. In some cases, multiple-choice and paired questions are very similar. As with paired choice questions, the reliability of the survey depends on your ability to provide appropriate choices. Sample A is an example of a multiple-choice question that provides choices that are so limited that it differs very little from a paired-choice question. Sample B provides broader options, which may produce much more valid results.

User Survey Sample – Multiple Choice

	Yes	No
Select the answer that best describes your experience.		
If a help link is available, I am likely to click on it.	○	○
The last time I clicked a help link the information provided was what I needed.	○	○
Help links are a good method for providing information.	○	○

FIGURE 4.1 Limited multiple choice.

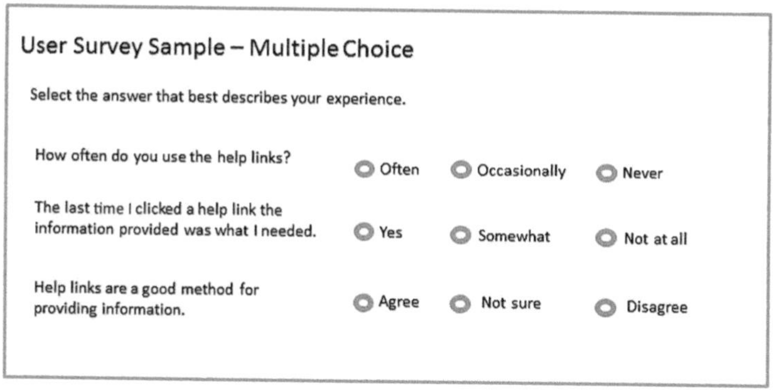

User Survey Sample – Multiple Choice

Select the answer that best describes your experience.

How often do you use the help links?   ◉ Often   ◉ Occasionally   ◉ Never

The last time I clicked a help link the
information provided was what I needed.   ◉ Yes   ◉ Somewhat   ◉ Not at all

Help links are a good method for
providing information.   ◉ Agree   ◉ Not sure   ◉ Disagree

FIGURE 4.2 Broader multiple choice.

Open-ended questions: While close-ended questions may be easier to analyze, they have their limitations inasmuch as they give participants only a narrow number of predetermined possible answers that may or may not reflect their ideas and preferences. For optimal results, a survey should also allow participants to answer some questions according to their own experiences. If your survey has a large number of participants, keep in mind that the feedback is valuable only if you have time to read and analyze it. When creating your personas, the comments participants make in the open-ended questions are often good quotes in the persona biographies.

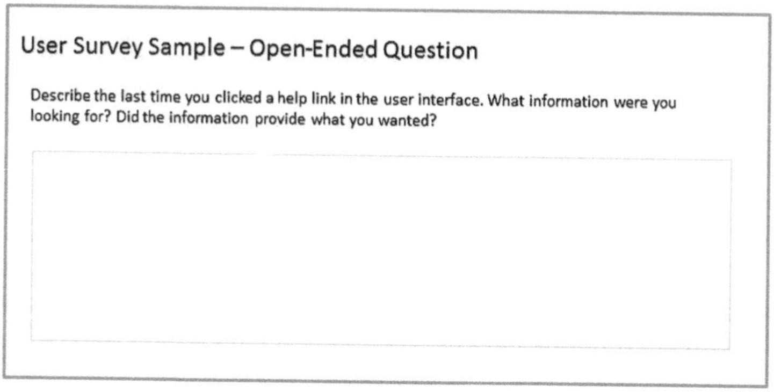

User Survey Sample – Open-Ended Question

Describe the last time you clicked a help link in the user interface. What information were you looking for? Did the information provide what you wanted?

There are many different ways you can deliver surveys; most often surveys are conducted either face to face or electronically.

Face-to-Face Surveys

The benefit of face-to-face surveys is that during the survey you can interact with the participants and take note of any additional comments and information they may provide while answering the survey questions. You can also answer any questions they may have regarding the survey, making sure they understand the rating scales and questions.

The downside of face-to-face surveys is that you may inadvertently influence the answers, thereby affecting the reliability of the survey. Because of the time needed in meeting each participant in person, the time investment per survey is much higher.

A less timely alternative is to complete the survey by telephone. This method provides the personal interaction, without requiring such a heavy time investment.

Online Surveys

In recent years, many good online survey applications, such as SurveyMonkey (surveymonkey.com), have been developed, offering low-cost basic services. Online surveys provide the easiest way to reach a large number of people: You set up the survey and send out the link via an e-mail; participants complete and submit the survey; and the online tool lets you collate and analyze the results.

The downsides of online surveys are their low response rates and their inability to offer personal interaction with your participants.

SITE VISITS

Site visits allow you to observe users in their own environment, providing insights into their everyday working practices and work environment. This is a good way to gather quantitative and qualitative information, assuming you have the necessary time and resources. If you are working on a business product, then your site visits will be to the company offices where your target users are located. Watching and observing them in that environment will help you understand how roles and work responsibilities interact and overlap in real-world situations. If you are working on a consumer product, seeing at first hand the varying skill levels and practices of different target segments will help you understand how real people interact with their desktop computers or mobile devices.

If possible, site visits should be made in pairs: One person on the team interacts with the participant, and the other takes notes.

Preparing for Site Visits

The first step in planning your site visits is to define the goals of the visits and then use the goals to create a list of questions to ask. While site visits allow for informal interaction and observation, having a list of questions prepared ahead of time will keep the conversation focused.

If you are conducting site visits at a corporation or business, learn about organization before your meeting. If you are conducting a home visit, call ahead of time to ask about the number of family members and their ages. Having basic information before arriving will help you plan and prepare the framework for your visit. Before the site visit, prepare a folder to take with you. The folder should include a tablet of paper, two pens or pencils, and your list of questions.

The Site Visit

Always arrive at the site on time with your site-visit folder. While you may find it easier to take notes on a laptop, it's not recommended during a site visit: You will be more attentive to the participant and will observe more if your focus is on the conversation rather than on the keyboard. If you are at the meeting alone, you may want to record the session. That way you can jot down observations, without worrying about missing important information. Never tape a session without explicit permission from the participant.

During the site visit, start by asking simple questions, leading up to the more probing questions. Ask for specific examples about the tasks the participants perform. Having them show you a typical workflow or sample of a task will result in better data than having them explain it to you. Ask the participants to describe the most common challenges and let them show you how they problem-solve along the way.

Only stay for the scheduled time period, and be sure to thank the participants when you leave.

After the Site Visit

After the session, it's advisable to write up your notes as soon as possible so that your observations and comments are fresh in your mind. If you went out as a pair, go over the notes together, not only to review the information gathered, but also to discuss ways to improve your process. Depending on the number of visits, you may decide to change the questions or the style of questioning after the first few visits.

And remember to send the participants an e-mail or note thanking them for their time.

FOCUS GROUPS

Focus groups were originally used by market researching teams but have now become a popular tool for development teams. The interaction among the groups provides a platform for participants to express their likes and dislikes, expectations, concerns, attitudes, and behaviors, and the groups are usually very happy to have a chance to impact an application or product.

Your first step in creating a focus group is to determine what information you are trying to gather and what you hope to learn. The group should consist of a small sample of target users—usually six to ten participants. When recruiting your participants, create your groups according to common roles and user tasks. Then, based on your needs, you should create a script, including the activities and the amount of time you will spend on each activity.

Activities can include round-table discussions, card-sorting exercises, problem solving, and reviews of sample applications and screens. For example, you might show the participants two sample screens and ask them to describe which one is preferable and why.

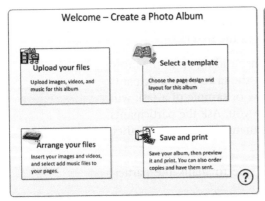

Then, you can introduce another sample, again asking the participants to compare the pages and discuss reasons why one may be preferable to another. When performing this activity with different groups, it's a good idea to switch the samples around to get more reliable feedback.

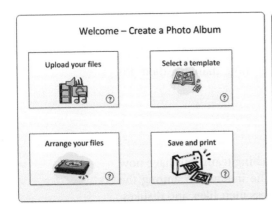

During the focus group session, you will need a moderator dedicated to facilitating the group discussions and activities. You'll also need at least one person to take notes.

The benefit of a focus group is that the group interaction stimulates the flow of ideas. Its disadvantage is that one or two strong personalities may monopolize the conversations; when this happens, you may end up with a group dynamic that inhibits the flow of ideas from the other participants. Occasionally, you may also find participants who exaggerate, or are less than truthful, affecting the reliability of the focus group results. It's important for the moderator to control the conversation, making sure everyone has a chance to speak, and to stay within the time limits allocated for each topic.

As with site visits, it's important to summarize your notes right away, while the experience and your recall of the comments is still fresh in your mind.

TALKING TO CUSTOMER SUPPORT

The customer support team is in direct contact with customers and usually has a deep understanding of users' needs and how users really work. The support team may also have detailed reports about support calls; this information will tell you what tasks users are trying to complete and the areas in the user interface where information is needed.

When gathering information from customer support, remember that while expert opinions are helpful, insights gathered from an informal conversation are not the same as empirical data. Asking specific questions about typical user tasks, scenarios, user work habits, and knowledge levels, and writing this information in a way that can be analyzed later will help you make the most of the data.

For example, these are some questions you may want to ask:

- What is the first task users perform when they open the application?
- What are the top three tasks users are performing when they call for help?
- Is there a specific step in each task where users get confused? What is the step, and what is the main cause of the confusion?
- What information will help the user understand what they need to complete that task successfully?

Asking questions in a way that elicits answers you can track and record makes it easier to analyze as data later.

GATHERING INFORMATION FROM THE INTERNET

The Internet can provide valuable information about the knowledge levels, real-life tasks, and information needs of your users. It can also help you understand the terminology your users are comfortable with when talking about the technologies associated with their tasks.

Viable sources of information on the Internet are newsgroups and support sites. These are sites where members of the product team, or other users such as product resellers, answer questions that have been posted by actual users. Reading the posts, their answers, and additional comments will familiarize you with typical user tasks, working environments, and the kind of information users are seeking. If your application hasn't been released yet, reading the posts for similar products will help you understand the types of issues your users may face later on. And if the information is posted in a way that can be measured and counted, you can create a chart or table showing the number of times a specific question or issue was raised.

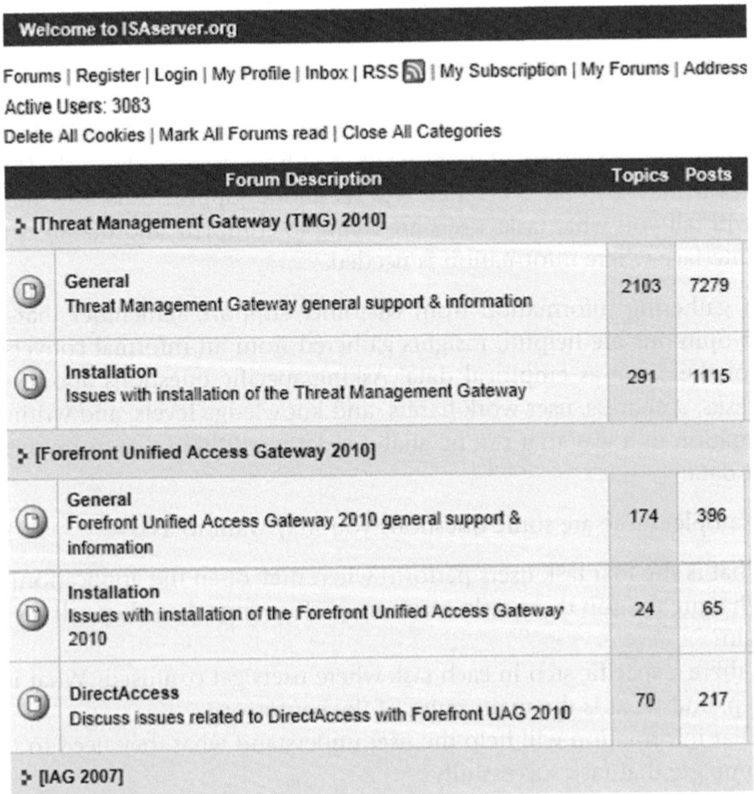

Welcome to ISAserver.org

Forums | Register | Login | My Profile | Inbox | RSS 🔊 | My Subscription | My Forums | Address
Active Users: 3083
Delete All Cookies | Mark All Forums read | Close All Categories

Forum Description	Topics	Posts
[Threat Management Gateway (TMG) 2010]		
General Threat Management Gateway general support & information	2103	7279
Installation Issues with installation of the Threat Management Gateway	291	1115
[Forefront Unified Access Gateway 2010]		
General Forefront Unified Access Gateway 2010 general support & information	174	396
Installation Issues with installation of the Forefront Unified Access Gateway 2010	24	65
DirectAccess Discuss issues related to DirectAccess with Forefront UAG 2010	70	217
[IAG 2007]		

FIGURE 4.3 Example of a forum log (isaserver.org).

If your product already has a support site, start by reading the posts on that site. If you see that users have similar questions or comments about a specific user task, this may indicate that the information accompanying an option or page in the user interface is not providing the right information, or that additional text clarifying expected or possible user actions is required. For example, the following posts show that users are frustrated trying to save an edited file, assuming that the feature is unavailable. If in fact the feature exists, but users cannot figure out how to find or use the feature, then you can surmise that users need better textual or visual cues for interacting with the application.

Theresa - November 1, 2012 - Motorola Photon 4G with version 1.0.13 ☜

★ ★ ★ ★ ★ **Sad**

This app currently doesn't allow me to edit the way I want to, and doesn't allow me to save an edited picture. There's no point in having it. I am going to delete the app.

Yen - October 28, 2012 - Version 1.0.13 ☜

★ ★ ★ ★ ★ **No save option, edit mode**

Edit mode is frustratingly USELESS, there's no option for saving edited photos. Kindly fix this ASAP

Khrys - October 30, 2012 - Samsung Galaxy Y with version 1.0.13 ☜

★ ★ ★ ★ ★ **save button :3**

how am i suppose to save pictures that i edited in "edit mode" if there's no save button :3

FIGURE 4.4 Example of online user posts.

In addition to learning about how users interact with the product, reading user posts will also help you understand their knowledge and motivation levels. While this may not be included as part of your data, it will help you understand user expectations and needs.

ANALYZING YOUR DATA

After gathering all your data, you'll need to make sense out of it. This requires interpretation, analysis, and categorization of the results. Following these general steps will help you organize the information in a way that is useful and will also help you understand how to best provide an information experience that meets your users' needs.

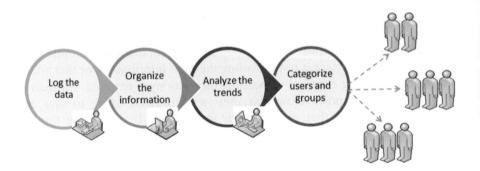

Your first step is to log the data. When using an online tool or computer application to create and distribute your surveys, the tool probably has a built-in feature for copying all your data into a central location. If your data was gathered manually, you will need to log it yourself. Fortunately, many programs are available to help you log data as well as organize and view the data. Microsoft Excel and e-survey are all examples of tools you can use to log and sort your data. The following example shows how logged data may be represented in a bar graph or pie chart. From this data, you can see that most respondents have a favorable opinion about inline help links.

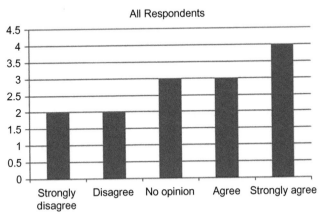

FIGURE 4.5 Respondents' answers to the question regarding the usefulness of inline help—graphical representation.

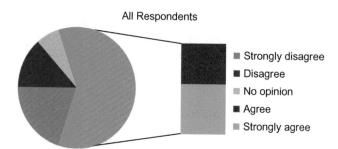

FIGURE 4.6 Respondents' answers to the question regarding the usefulness of inline help—graphical representation.

Your next step is to organize your data, looking at demographics and user attributes. By analyzing the data further, the results provide another level of information, allowing you to draw conclusions about specific user groups. For example, you can see that system administrators have a more favorable opinion of inline help links, while support desk administrators responses were less favorable.

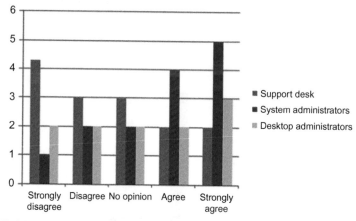

FIGURE 4.7 Example of responses across groups.

If you wanted to analyze this even further, you can divide the user groups into subgroups, based on relevant demographics, such as age and experience, or specific tasks.

In a consumer product, it may be relevant to examine how different age groups or genders respond to questions. For example, if we go back to the questions we asked above about user interaction and attitudes toward online help links, this is a sample of how that data may be presented, if you wanted to see how respondents answer a single question.

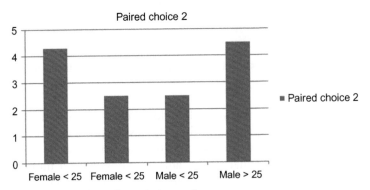

FIGURE 4.8 Example of data for a single question.

Organizing your data visually, using charts and graphs, will help you understand the data, making it easier to see the relationships between responses and to draw conclusions.

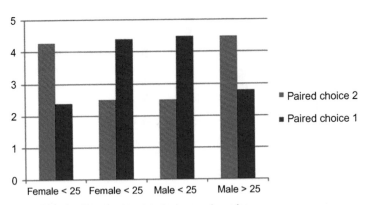

FIGURE 4.9 Sample of comparing data for age and gender.

After you log and organize your data, it's time to start analyzing it. The tools will help you organize the information, but you will still need to decide what it all means and how to use it. Ultimately, the tools you decide to use will be determined by the depth of the statistical analysis you deem necessary and the amount of time you want to invest.

In most cases, basic statistical analysis and simple tools such as PowerPoint and Excel can be used to express your data visually. The charts and graphs offered by simple and easy-to-use tools are generally sufficient for understanding user trends. If you have a lot of data, you may feel overwhelmed with information. It therefore helps to start by looking at the big picture, finding trends across demographics, user tasks, and user goals.

When looking at each piece of data, and analyzing the information you've gathered, think about how that data will ultimately help you create a better information experience for your customers.

After you analyze your data and see trends across demographics, you can categorize the users into groups. These groups become the basis for defining customer personas. Creating personas and persona biographies is a good tool for mapping information needs to real users. This will help you understand the kind of information they need and how your user interface text can best serve their purposes.

SUMMARY

Before creating the information for your users, you'll need to understand what kind of information they need and the tasks they will perform. Simple research methodologies can be used to gather and analyze your data, helping you define user groups and understand your users.

- The steps involved in gathering data about your users are as follows: Plan your research methodology, implement your plan, analyze the data, and then use the information to create user groups for your personas.
- Surveys are a good tool for gathering measurable data from a large sample of potential users.
- Site visits let you observe users in their natural environment, which helps you understand their real work habits and needs.
- Focus groups provide feedback from a small group of sample users, helping you learn about user preferences, expectations, and behaviors.
- Talking to customer support can help you understand what tasks users are trying to perform, and their user scenarios.
- When looking at your data, think about how that data will ultimately help you create a better information experience for your customers.

CHAPTER 5

Creating Your Personas

INTRODUCTION

In the previous chapters, you learned about different types of users and applications, and methods for learning about the preferences of users who may be interacting with your application. As you gathered your data, such as demographic information, as well as your users likes and dislikes, you were also learning how users work and the types of tasks they perform. All the data you gathered helps identify key characteristics and similarities across users, so that you can group and categorize them. These groups and categories become the basis for deriving your target personas. Your application may have several personas, each based on the specific characteristics and attributes of a major user group for your application.

Although personas are fictional characters, the data used to create them is based on real-life people who exemplify your target user groups. After identifying your personas, you'll create persona biographies, including a name, picture, and title of the persona. The biography includes background information relevant to the application, such as experience, skills, and motivation. Then, you'll describe the tasks and goals of the user, relevant personal information, and motivational factors. Taking into account needs, abilities, motivation levels, key tasks, goals, and use-case scenarios of your customers will help you deliver the content your users want and need, in a way that makes sense to them.

Personas can be created in several ways, depending on what you already know about your users.

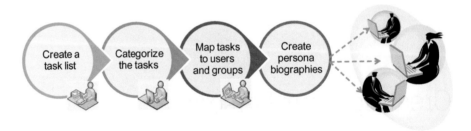

If you have already identified your main user groups, you can start by creating a task list for each user group. For example, in a home banking application, you may have identified three main groups of users: users who do all their banking online, users who only check their bank statements and transfer funds when needed, and users who mainly make stock purchases and sales. Then, you can create a list of tasks for each group. If you haven't identified your main user groups or target users, then you can start by creating a task list mapping them to user groups later on in the process.

CREATING THE TASK LIST

The task list comprises all the tasks you expect users will perform with the application. These are the tasks for which the application is being, or was, designed to support. Let's say for example, you are working on an application users will want to download for tracking daily exercise and calorie intake. This is a sample of what a task list for this application may include:

Tasks
Create user account
Log in using the user account
Enter personal details (date of birth, sex, etc.,)
Enter height
Enter weight
Calculate BMI
Enter target weight
Calculate calories needed per day to reach target weight
Enter activities (calories burned throughout the day)
View food calorie lists
Join an exercise chat group
Find friends to participate in chat group
Log into chat group
Create weekly exercise schedule
Create daily vitamin chart
Create weekly menu

Continued...

Continued
Tasks
View daily reports
View weekly reports
View monthly reports

At this point, you don't need to identify the subtasks or to create a task analysis of each step comprising the tasks. As you create your list of tasks, for each task ask yourself the following questions:

- What kind of user group is this task most relevant for?
- Why does the user perform this task (what is the main goal)?
- When does the user perform this task?
- How frequently is this task performed by the user?
- Is this task core to the application?

After creating your task list, you are ready to categorize the tasks. Thinking about these questions will help you create the task categories.

CATEGORIZING USER TASKS

There are several ways to categorize tasks, and each task often belongs to more than one category. The categories below are consistent across most applications, although you may find you have additional categories that are important for your application.

Proactive versus Reactive Tasks

When a user initiates a task of his or her own volition, it is a proactive task. When a user performs a task due to an event or outside occurrence, the task is considered to be reactive. For example, making a phone call is a proactive task, whereas answering the call is reactive. In a business application, typical tasks, such as installing and configuring the application, are proactive tasks. Responding to program events or issues are reactive tasks. A reactive task can also be a response to a system notification or message that comes through an application (such as update notifications, or reply from another user of an interactive program).

Understanding the difference between these types of tasks is important when you are deciding where and how to deliver the information, and how much information users need while interacting with the application. Users initiating a proactive task may be willing to spend time reading or searching for information prior to starting a task; users responding to an event or error want the information available and within their reach at a specific moment.

Task Frequency

Another variable to consider when categorizing your tasks is how frequently users will perform that task. Task frequency can be broken down into three main levels:

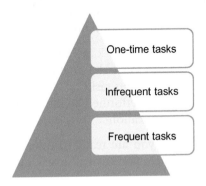

One-time tasks are those tasks users perform once, generally when downloading or installing an application, and when configuring initial settings. After the task is done, users will rarely, if ever, need to repeat the task. While this may make the task seem insignificant, if all your users must perform a task, and it is core to the application, then it's important to make sure all your users can successfully complete the task.

Infrequent tasks are those tasks users perform more than once, but not on a regular basis. For example, in the accompanying list, users will probably modify their weight setting as they lose or gain weight. But only some users—the ones who may still growing—will modify the height setting as well.

Frequent tasks are those tasks users perform many times throughout the life cycle of the product—sometimes several times during the day, once daily, or even weekly. For example, in the list, entering food intake will be done frequently at the end of each day, or throughout the day, if the application is being used as intended.

Understanding task frequency will help you focus on tasks that have higher relevance for users and on tasks that require the most readily available information.

Core Tasks and Noncore Tasks

Another way to categorize tasks is by level of importance. Tasks that most, if not all users, regardless of their expertise, will complete are core tasks (these are also known as basic tasks). These tasks are pivotal to the application—and being able to easily understand and complete core casks is crucial for users to successfully interact with and use your application. In our example above, a core or basic task is entering exercise data and tracking calories burned per exercise. Noncore and advanced tasks are tasks that only users with a certain level of knowledge, skills, or confidence are interested in trying to use.

Software development teams usually consider the 80/20 rule when designing software. In short, this rule says that 20 percent of your features are the most used and interacted with. These are the tasks that are considered core, or basic, to the application.

When designing your information, and planning the text that appears in the user interface, identifying and keeping in mind these tasks—the 20 percent— and mapping them to the target personas will help you focus on providing the right experience for the text most users will actually rely on when interacting with the application.

Keep in mind that noncore tasks are not necessarily advanced. In fact, they may be rather simple to use and understand and may be important for the overall success of your application, but just not crucial for interacting with the application.

First-Time User Experience Tasks

Getting users over the initial first-time experience is a challenge in many applications. The first-time experience may include the download (or install), sign-up, and login phase. But when planning your information experience and content, the first-time experience refers to the point where users begin interacting with the application to complete tasks. If the first-time experience is difficult in an online application, users may simply close the application and move on to an easier one. In our example above, the first-time experience would include entering the personal details, such as birthdate, height, weight, and weight goal. It would also include the first time the user tries to enter a food item or activity. Adding a simple tutorial, help callouts, or inline text may provide the additional support users need to get over the initial learning curve.

In the next sample, the inline text provides all the information the first-time user needs to use the calculator.

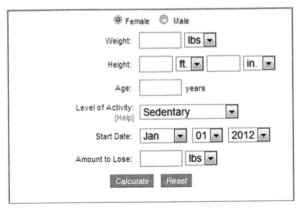

Weight Loss Target Date Calculator

Do you have 20lbs to lose? 30lbs? More? The **Weight Loss Target Date** calculator gives you an idea of how long it will take to lose that weight. After you enter your info, the calculator estimates how many calories you need to stay at the same weight (total daily calorie needs). It then calculates 5 different calorie deficits and how long it will take you to lose those pounds.

(If you want to calculate your total weight loss percentage, use the Weight Loss Percentage calculator.)

Instructions:

1) Enter your current weight, height, age, and activity level, as well as your start date for losing weight and the number of pounds (or kilos) you want to lose.

2) Click "Calculate."

3) The Weight Loss Table gives you 5 options to choose from. Pick the one you feel most comfortable with.

- **Option 1:** 500 calories less than your total daily calorie needs. (approx. 1lb a week -- add in more exercise to burn more calories)
- **Option 2:** 15% less than your total daily calorie needs. (slow but steady)
- **Option 3:** 20% calories less than your total daily calorie needs. (average loss)
- **Option 4:** 25% calories less than your total daily calorie needs.(moderate)
- **Option 5:** 30% calories less than your total daily calorie needs. (aggressive)

Note: This calculator will not go below 1200 calories a day for women and 1800 calories a day for men.

FIGURE 5.1 Providing inline help (FitWatch.com).

In a business application, the first-time user experience may consist of defining initial configuration settings. In this case, users are more motivated to succeed, but a difficult experience may result in calls to customer support that cost the company time and money. Understanding your users will help you decide how to help them through the experience by providing, for example, a well-designed landing page, or wizard.

Understanding the tasks involved and the difficulties different types of users experience during their initial interaction with the application will help you integrate a helpful information experience into the user workflow for each target persona, getting them over the initial learning curve.

MAPPING TASKS AND CATEGORIES TO TARGET USERS

After categorizing your tasks, the next step is to create a mapping between the tasks, the categorization, and the target users. Let's assume that after gathering our data, we identified four user groups for our exercise application. Each of these user groups becomes the basis for at least one persona.

- Women ages 30 and up who are trying to lose weight, get back in shape, and eat more healthily. This includes women who have recently given birth. We will call this persona Monica.
- Men ages 18−35 who are interested in staying in shape, strength training, and eating the foods they need for increasing muscle mass. We will call this persona Jordan.
- Men ages 35 and up who are trying to lose weight, and begin an exercise program after years of little or no exercise regime. We will call this persona Albert.
- Teenagers ages 15−18 who are interested in maintaining or losing weight and keeping healthy. We will call this persona Kim.

As soon as you decide on names for your personas, it's a good idea to start using them in team conversations, written specifications, and design reviews. Ask questions about the personas, such as "Is this something Jordan already knows how to do?" and "How frequently will Monica need to do this?" Using personas in this way will help keep them at the center of discussions and hopefully in the center of the design decisions. It will also help you map your information design and text to real user-tasks and goals.

Your mapping can be done simply in a table, or you can use a graphics program to create a chart. The mapping for the exercise program may look something like this.

Tasks	Type	Frequency	Target Persona
Create user account	Core	Infrequent/First time only	All
Log in using the user account	Core	Frequent/First time	All
Password reset	Noncore	Infrequent	All
Enter personal details— birthday	Core	First time/One time	All
Enter personal details, height, and weight	Core	First time/One time	All
Calculating BMI	Core	Infrequent	All
Update height details	Core	Infrequent	Kim
Update weight details	Core	Frequent	All

Continued...

Continued			
Tasks	**Type**	**Frequency**	**Target Persona**
Input body measurements	Core	Infrequent	All
Enter exercise goals	Noncore/ Advanced	Infrequent	Kim/Jordan
Enter exercises done (time and activity)	Core	Frequent	All
Calculate calorie equivalents per exercise	Core	Frequent	All
Joining an exercise chat group	Noncore	Infrequent	Kim/Jordan/Albert
Logging into a chat group to read the latest posts	Noncore	Frequent (for chat group user)	Kim/Jordan/Albert
Entering posts to the chat group	Noncore	Frequent Nonfrequent	Kim/Jordan/Albert
Compete with other players in chat group	Noncore/ Advanced	Infrequent	Kim/Jordan
Creating weekly exercise schedule	Core	Infrequent	Jordan/Albert/ Monica
Enter vitamin intake	Noncore/ Advanced	Frequent	Kim/Jordan
Create weekly menu	Noncore	Infrequent	Jordan/Albert/ Monica
Create daily reports	Noncore	Infrequent	Jordan/Monica
Create weekly reports	Noncore	Infrequent	Jordan/Albert/ Monica
Create monthly reports	Noncore	Infrequent	Jordan/Albert
View reports	Noncore	Frequent	All

CREATING USER SCENARIOS

Once you have created your mappings, you can use the information to create scenarios for each persona. Scenarios describe how the application is used to meet the real-life needs of users. If you have done your research correctly and have created your task list, then your scenarios should map to the personas you identified, and you should be able to string together your tasks to create a story, or stories, about your users and their interaction with the application. For example, using our above sample, we can create a scenario for Monica.

SAMPLE DAILY SCENARIO: MONICA

Every morning after weighing herself, Monica logs into the exercise tool on her laptop computer. First, she enters her current weight and compares it to the previous day's weight. Next, Monica runs on the treadmill for 20 minutes, showers, and rushes off to work. Sitting at her desk, she logs back into the tool, this time on her smartphone. She updates the tool to add her treadmill time to her daily exercise log. She also adds the 10-minute walk from the car to the office. Monica navigates to the calorie counter feature and enters the items she had for breakfast. Throughout the day she updates the calorie counter to include all her meals and snacks. She also updates the exercise tracking feature to include any additional exercise, such as walking her dog and walking up four flights of stairs to her office. At the end of the day, Monica checks to see if she expended as many, or more, calories than she consumed.

Every Sunday, Monica prepares a food plan for the coming week. She would like to join one of the chat groups, but she is not sure how to join.

Monica is one persona; other personas may have different daily tasks. For example, Albert, who is becoming an avid cyclist, may want to compare his speed and distance on his morning ride to his own previous performance and to that of other cyclists. Participating in a cyclist chat group would be a frequent task for him.

SAMPLE DAILY SCENARIO: ALBERT

Albert rushes to work in the morning and has breakfast in the office canteen. He is busy all day at work and usually grabs a sandwich for lunch.

When he gets home from work early, three days a week, he gets on his bicycle and rides 5 miles before dinner. After dinner he sits in front of his computer and if he remembers he enters the exercise details into the tool. He also tries to remember what he ate and logs that as well. He checks his e-mail and sees that his cycling group is riding on Saturday for 20 miles, so he enters that into the tool as well. Then he sees that the cycling chat group had some activity going on since he last checked, so he logs into the chat group to read the latest posts. Someone has asked a question about a bike trail he is familiar with, so he answers the question and adds information to a few other comments.

Albert doesn't weigh himself regularly, so he only updates the weight field every few weeks.

Jordan, is somewhat of an exercise fanatic and is very interested in tracking his progress. This is what his scenario may look like:

SAMPLE DAILY SCENARIO: JORDAN

Jordan gets up and goes through his morning exercise routine. When he is dressed and ready for work, he makes himself a protein shake for breakfast and plans his day. As he drinks breakfast, he plans his exercise routine for the day and enters the exercise activities into the tool. He checks the vitamin plan and takes the vitamins he has listed for that day.

On his way home from work, he stops off at the gym and runs on the treadmill for 30 minutes; then he goes through the weight-training circuit he created with his trainer.

At the end of the day, he reviews the exercise activities he entered into the tool, and updates any changes. He also logs the food intake for his day and notes the percentage of protein, carbohydrates and fat. Since he weighed himself at the gym, he also updates his weight if there were changes and checks the effect on his BMI.

While he eats dinner, Jordan checks the chat group to see if there are any interesting posts.

CREATING THE PERSONA BIOGRAPHIES

When you have completed mapping the tasks, it's time to put all the information together and create your persona biographies. The persona biography should include the persona name and short biography, and how the data relates to your goals.

The following samples show how personas for the task list shown in the previous pages may be defined. You can see that the relevant demographic information is provided, as are the goals of the user and their information needs. Also, keep in mind that you may create biographies for all the personas you identified, or you can select the top few.

Sample Biographies

Monica

Age: 55
Status: Married + 2 children
Occupation: Sales Trainer

Goals: Lose 10 pounds she gained and to improve her overall health

Primary tasks:
- Track calories consumed and burned throughout the day
- Track weight loss and improved BMI

How she uses the application:
- Monica accesses the tool throughout the day, mainly on her tablet device. She also users her smartphone when at work.
- She enters her morning weight and then enters each food item consumed throughout the day.
- She enters all activity done throughout the day, including her walk to and from the bus.
- She often searches for caloric and nutritional information before purchasing food items
- She plans her weekly diet using the built in food planner

Information needs:
- Monica likes help callout and getting started pages
- She reads and responds to notifications
- She would click help links on a tablet, but not on a smartphone

Quote: I want a tool that helps me stay on track and is easy to use. I think it would be fun to join a chat group for support, but I don't know how.

FIGURE 5.2 Sample persona: women ages 30 and up trying to lose weight.

Albert N.

Age: 47
Status: Divorced
Occupation: Supervisor

Goals: Get into better shape and improve eating habits

Primary tasks:
- Track exercise, mainly cycling which he took up recently.
- Track weight loss and improved BMI.

How he uses the application:
- Accesses the tool on his desktop computer.
- Enters his exercise when he is in front of the computer.
- Enters planned cycling events into the tool.
- Recently joined the cycling chat group and participates in the chat sessions when he has time.
- He participated in one challenge, and wants to do it again.
- Checks his weekly and monthly progress when he remembers.

Information needs:
- Reads the text labels and prompts. Prefers his laptop since it is easier to read and input data than a smart phone.
- Doesn't read the help. But reads help callouts and messages.
- Responds to notifications.

Quote: I want to learn what else I can do with this tool. I am not sure what other features are available.

FIGURE 5.3 Sample persona men ages 35 and up trying to lose weight.

Jordan L.

Age: 25
Status: Single
Occupation: History Teacher

Goals: Increase fitness level and increase muscle mass

Primary tasks:
- Track exercise done throughout the day
- Make sure he's eating the right foods and quantities for his workout regime

How he uses the application:
- Accesses his tool on his smartphone and on his laptop
- Creates a weekly workout schedule and enters the details of each workout.
- Tracks calories consumed, as well as protein and carbohydrates
- Records vitamin intake
- Belongs to a chat group inside the tool. Check the messages daily, but infrequently contributes.
- Checks his weekly and monthly progress

Information needs:
- Wants the tool to be self explanatory. Will not click help links.
- Reads button labels and prompts, and responds to notifications

Quote: I want a tool that shows me how I'm progressing, and is easy and fun to use.

FIGURE 5.4 Sample persona men ages 18—35 interested in strength training.

After creating your persona biographies, make copies to hand out to the team and post them where they are clearly visible. As you create the information designs and write your text, refer back to them, asking yourself what information each user needs, and the best way to provide it to them.

SUMMARY

Personas can be created in several ways. You can work in this flow: Create a task list, categorize the tasks, map tasks to users and group, and then create your persona biographies.

- The tasks list is comprised of all the tasks *you expect users will perform with the application.*
- Tasks can be proactive or reactive. When a user initiates a task of his or her own volition, it is a proactive task. When a user performs a task due to an event or outside occurrence, it's considered a reactive task.
- Task frequency refers to how often the task is performed: Once, infrequently, or frequently.
- Core tasks are tasks most, if not all, users will complete when using the application.
- Getting users over the first-time experience is important as it sets expectations for the user.
- Mapping your tasks to personas helps you understand the priorities for each user group.
- User scenarios describe how the application is used to meet the needs of your users.
- The persona biography should include the persona name and a short biography, and show how the data relates to your goals.
- After creating your personas, refer back to them when creating your information.

Designing Your Information Experience Strategy

Because users come from a variety of backgrounds and levels, there is no "one-size-fits-all" information experience. What is apparent and intuitive to one user may be difficult and complex to another, less experienced user. Understanding your users and their tasks is paramount in building a successful strategy.

Once you understand your users, it's time to think about their information needs and how the information will be delivered. This section describes the components for creating a successful IX strategy. This includes understanding the product life cycle and selecting the best information delivery mechanism based on the immediate needs of the end user.

CHAPTER 6

Understanding User Reading Patterns

INTRODUCTION

In recent years, marketing and usability teams have spent millions of dollars and countless hours trying to understand how users view online pages. This data is used to decide where advertisements are placed in a page, to prepare general page layouts, and to show what fonts and colors are used in a page. This research can help writers design how to create the information in the page and how users read the information. The end result of these activities help our users interact with our products.

Traditional research methods, such as usability studies, site visits, and user observation, also provide insights into how layout and content affect the way users read web pages, dialogs, wizards, and the like provided within an application. By taking the information learned from research and applying it together with basic usability principles, you can create user interface text that provides the optimal user experience.

HOW DO USERS INTERACT WITH ONLINE TEXT?

Most recent research on how users read online text has been done on web pages, using marketing research to observe and improve web page design. Advanced research methodologies include using tools such as eye tracking and mouse tracking, which provide empirical data and analytics about user navigation and interaction with the elements within the surfaces of online pages.

Eye-Tracking Research

Eye tracking as a means of understanding user interaction with a product and improving product design was first used in the 1950s to study the movement of pilots' eyes as they landed an airplane. It wasn't until the 1980s that researchers became interested in applying eye-tracking technology for understanding human–computer interaction. During an eye-tracking study, the user wears an eye-tracking apparatus, which includes an eye camera and other optical equipment, mounted on a helmet or some other headband, placed on the user's head. Following an initial calibration stage, the apparatus records user eye movements as they navigate through each task, tracking both the pupil and cornea reflection as the user views the page.

The eye-tracking data provides a visual assessment about how a user interacts with an interface, showing how a user interacts with specific areas on the page. As an additional form of data, eye-tracking software also records eye movements and mouse clicks, helping researchers understand the correlation between the user's eye movements, gaze patterns, and actions. This data provides insights into the user's viewing patterns, and while they can't show you what users are thinking as they look at a screen, they can provide some insights.

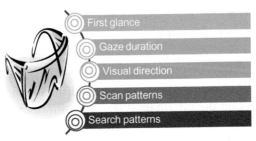

The information provided by eye-tracking research helps us understand the ways users view and interact with online pages.

- First glance: The area on the page that first catches the user's attention
- Gaze duration: How long users gaze on a particular area
- Visual direction: How users visually move through the user interface

- Scan patterns: How users scan pages and read text
- Search patterns: How users scan pages when searching for specific items

Through analysis of eye-tracking visualizations and recorded user mouse movement, results can easily be correlated and interpreted. For application designers, the data helps determine where to place the most important options and buttons. For information designers, the visualizations can show you where to place text that is most relevant and how much text users are likely to read in different locations on a page. Analysis tools provided in the eye-tracking software can further show you how users scan and read your text.

Only a few years ago, eye-tracking technology required users to wear a heavy helmet-like structure and heavy glasses. This made it difficult for users to feel and act natural during the eye-tracking sessions. In recent years, eye-tracking technology has improved considerably, with portable units and smaller glasses held in place with a headband. This helps users feel more at ease and provides better results. While lightweight headbands and smaller glasses allow users to move about more freely, users are still aware of the equipment on their heads and are conscious that their eye movements are being observed.

There are two common ways to show the visual output of an eye-tracking test: heat maps and gaze plots.

Heat Maps

A heat map is a graphical representation using colors to show where activity takes place, based on duration of gaze. When used to evaluate user interfaces, darker colors, such as red, usually indicate areas with lower activity, and brighter colors (such as orange, yellow, and green) show areas with highest activity. Areas with no coloration have no activity. For example, the accompanying graphic shows how users viewed this web page. Most attention is paid to the box on the left side of the page, with very little visual activity on the right side of the page. You can also see that visual activity is strongest at the top of the page, becoming weaker toward the bottom of the page.

FIGURE 6.1 Example of a heat map (Tobii Eye-Tracking Software).

In his book, *Eyetracking Web Usability*, Jakob Nielson identifies users' tendency to view a page in an F pattern and to focus their attention on information presented in bulleted lists. This page, taken from Jakob Nielson's research, shows a typical F pattern, which is similar to the pattern shown in the preceding example.

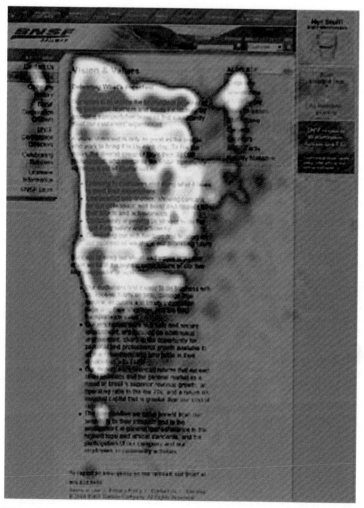

FIGURE 6.2 Example of a heat map (Jakob Nielson and Kara Pernice, *Eyetracking Web Usability*, 2009).

Gaze Plots

Gaze plots provide a visualization of user search patterns, showing an optical mapping of user scanning behavior in order. For example, the accompanying gaze plot shows the search pattern of a user when presented with a new web page. Similar to the outcome of the preceding heat map you can see that most activity occurs on the left side, toward the top of the page, with little or no activity toward the bottom right corner of the screen.

**LABORATORY OF COMPUTER
AND INFORMATION SCIENCE**
ADAPTIVE INFORMATICS
RESEARCH CENTRE

| Home | Contact | Research | Teaching | People | Jobs | Demos | Software |

Research and education at CIS

The Laboratory of Computer and Information Science (CIS) is one of the laboratories of the Department of Computer Science and Engineering at the Helsinki University of Technology.

The mission of the laboratory is to conduct research and provide education in the area of **adaptive informatics**.

By adaptive informatics we mean a field of research where automated learning algorithms are used to discover the relevant informative concepts, components, and their mutual relations from large amounts of data.

Adaptivity enables computers to adapt to the needs of individuals, groups, enterprises and organizations in the changing world.

Interfacing with the continuously **growing amounts** of data in scientific, medical, industrial, and financial fields and their transformation to intelligible form for the human user is one of our main foci. Techniques that can quickly discover and analyze complex patterns and learn from new data will be indispensable for information-intensive applications.

The research of the CIS laboratory is concentrated within two Centres of Excellence: the Adaptive Informatics Research Centre and the Pattern Discovery group of the From Data to Knowledge Research Unit.

We offer undergraduate and post-graduate studies on our research fields with the goal of educating knowledgeable, skillful and reflective practitioners and researchers for the field. Our majors are Computer and Information Science, Bioinformatics and Language Technology.

Research highlights

News

- Haku Teknilliseen korkeakouluun on alkanut 1.3. Tulisitko opiskelemaan informaatiotekniikkaa?
- Labran avoimet ovet opiskelijoille ma 12.3.2007 12-16
- Postdoc position in machine learning and bioinformatics
- Two new Master's Programmes, one in bioinformatics (MBI) and another in Machine Learning and Data Mining (Macadamia) will start in the autumn of 2007. The application deadline for both was January 31.

Local information

There is information for members and visitors of the lab on the local pages, which are accessible only from within the lab.

You are at **CIS** → Home page
Page maintained by webmaster at cis.hut.fi, last updated Friday, 24-Feb-2006 11:51:52 EET

Google      Google Search

○ WWW ⦿ www.cis.hut.fi   Tracking by Tobii

STUDY: Webbiselailua.   STIMULUS: GoogleFi.   RECORDING: 1.   FRAME: http://www.cis.hut.fi/.
TIME SEGMENT: Only include fixations inside interval [39571,55274] ms.

FIGURE 6.3 Sample gaze plot (AALTO, School of Statistical Machine Learning and Bioinformatics).

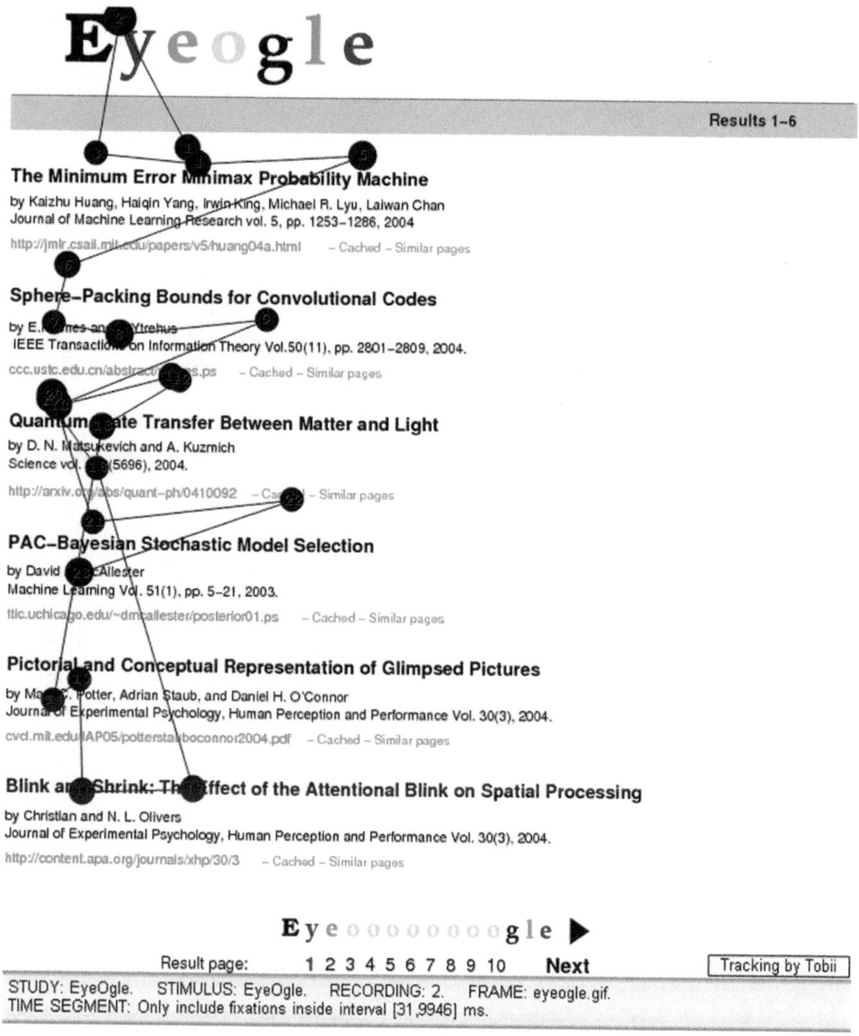

FIGURE 6.4 Sample gaze plot (AALTO, School of Statistical Machine Learning and Bioinformatics).

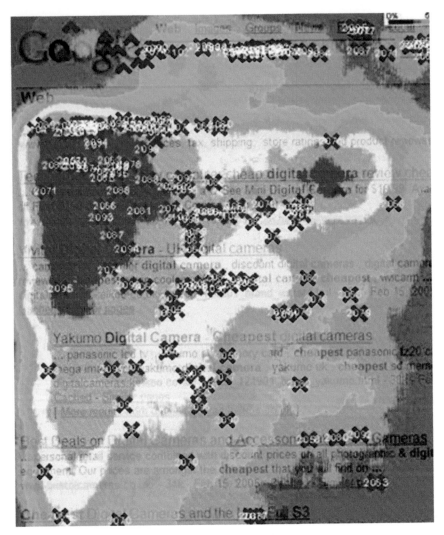

FIGURE 6.5 Heat map for Google.com.

Research showing how users view a page on Google.com shows similar viewing patterns to the above heat maps.

The following example shows the comparison between the heat map and gaze plot for this page. When combined, you can see how comparing heat maps and gaze plots can show you how users moved around the page and viewed the page.

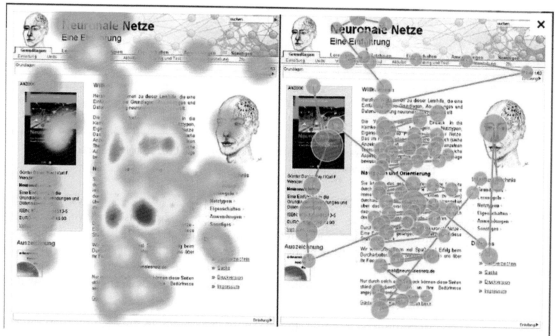

FIGURE 6.6 Example of a heat map and the corresponding gaze plot
(Courtesy of Günter Daniel Rey).

Gaze plots can also be configured to show how users read text. This helps you understand how users scan blocks of text provided on a page. As you can see in this example, users start at the top left and read in a zig-zag pattern. However, toward the bottom of the text, the pattern stops with users only glancing at words toward the bottom of the text.

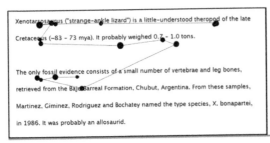 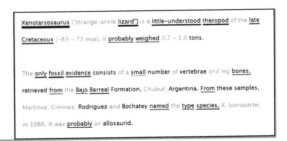

FIGURE 6.7 Example of how users scan text from (AALTO, School of Statistical Machine Learning and Bioinformatics).

Mouse-Tracking Research

Mouse tracking, as its name implies, shows how users move the mouse around the page, and where and how frequently they click various options. Mouse-tracking heat maps are similar to any other heat map, showing areas where users most frequently moved the mouse or most often clicked. Mouse-tracking data is also useful for identifying "dead zones," that is, the areas that have little or no activity.

The following example shows a mouse heat map. In the example, you can see where users moved the mouse most frequently, other areas where mouse movement was detected, and areas where users did not interact with the page.

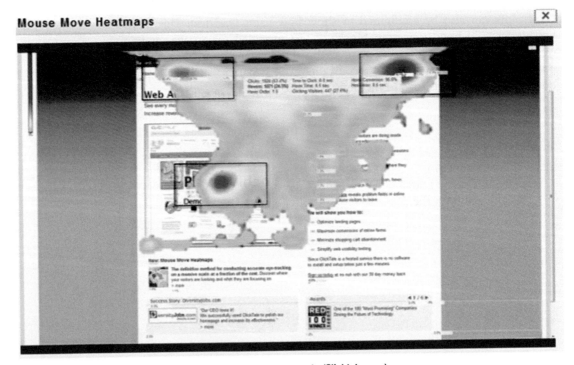

FIGURE 6.8 Sample mouse movements (Clicktale.com).

Click heat maps show the places on the page where users clicked the mouse. In the example below, you can see which options were most frequently clicked by users and areas where users did not have any interaction.

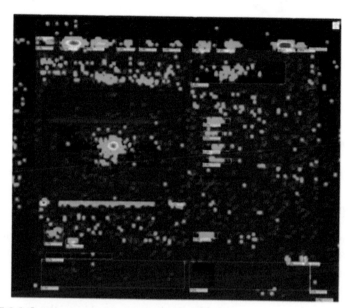

FIGURE 6.9 Sample mouse click frequency (Clicktale.com).

While mouse click data helps you understand which areas have the most activity, in the absence of other research you have no real way of telling *why* users clicked those options and avoided clicking others. Specifically, you can't tell if users gazed at an area but did not click the option, or if they did not view the area at all. As such, mouse click tracking alone provides limited value. However, mouse click tracking, when combined with eye tracking or other research methods, is a powerful tool for understanding the correlation between how users search a page and how they interact with the links and options available in the page. For example, this chart shows the eye-tracking pattern, up until the time the user clicked an item.

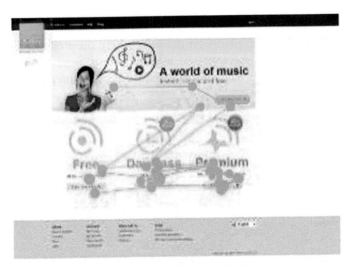

FIGURE 6.10 Gaze plot pattern and mouse interaction (Tobii.com).

WHAT THE RESEARCH TELLS US

Fortunately, because the research shows that there is a high correlation (84 to 88 percent) between eye-tracking and mouse-tracking movements, the combination of both mediums is considered solid evidence and provides many insights into how users read text presented on a screen.

Based on this research—eye tracking and mouse tracking—the research community has reached a general consensus about the way users search for and interact with user interfaces, and how they read text online.[1]

Using the conclusions of Nielson's research and based on what we know about how users read online text, here is a simple list of guidelines you should consider when building information into the user interface:

- Users start reading at the top left corner of the page and move horizontally, in an F formation (this is the opposite for right-to-left languages).
- After reading the first or second line of text on a page, users begin scanning the text.
- Users scan text looking at keywords or phrases that will help them complete the task at hand. They do not read word by word, or read entire blocks of text. Rather, they are looking for relevant bits of information.

---

[1]Many well-known research findings in web usability were presented by Jakob Nielson (Nielsen, (2006)), and many designers and writers use his research as the basis for web site design.

- Users are more likely to read bulleted lists than blocks of text.
- Users make a selection on the page as soon as they think they have enough information to understand the options. This is the point when they stop reading or skimming the text.
- Users rarely, if ever, focus on the bottom right corner of the page.

Based on these conclusions from the research, here are some helpful guidelines for writing user interface text:

- Provide the most important or useful pieces of information at the top of the page. If you have information the user must know before doing anything else on the page, it should be in the first line of text or set apart from another block of text.
- Make the text easy to scan. Start a sentence with the main point of the sentence and use concise language throughout.
- Avoid large blocks of text. Instead, use bullet points, or callouts.
- Break your content into meaningful chunks of information in order to help users scan it for the information they need. Keep in mind that long lines of text are hard to scan.
- Be aware that the words you use will help users find information as they skim through the page. Make sure keywords are easy to locate within the text.
- To help users understand the relationship between text and interactive elements, maintain visual proximity between text and corresponding options.

READABILITY SCALES

Although placement on the page strongly affects how users read online, reading level is another factor you should consider when designing and creating your text.

Many factors affect reading level, such as the user's reading skills and knowledge levels, but there are many readability scales and formulas available for determining the ease with which the average reader can read and understand your text. Most readability formulas are based on one syntactic variable (word length) and one semantic variable (number of words in a sentence).

The most common methods for evaluating reading ease are the Flesch–Kincaid Grade Level Scale and the Flesch–Kincaid Reading Ease Scale, which are available in most word processors, such as Microsoft Word.

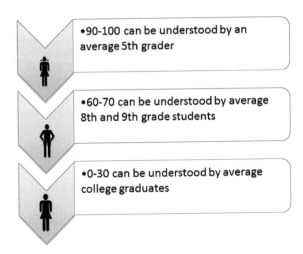

- •90-100 can be understood by an average 5th grader
- •60-70 can be understood by average 8th and 9th grade students
- •0-30 can be understood by average college graduates

FIGURE 6.11 Reading Ease Scale.

This is how Microsoft Word presents readability statistics for the first sentence in this page:

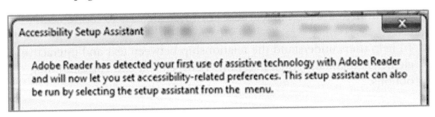

Accessibility Setup Assistant

Adobe Reader has detected your first use of assistive technology with Adobe Reader and will now let you set accessibility-related preferences. This setup assistant can also be run by selecting the setup assistant from the menu.

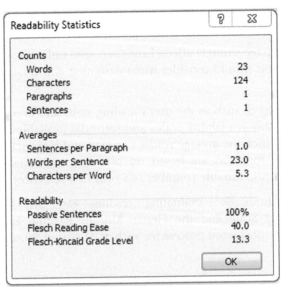

Readability Statistics

Counts	
Words	23
Characters	124
Paragraphs	1
Sentences	1
Averages	
Sentences per Paragraph	1.0
Words per Sentence	23.0
Characters per Word	5.3
Readability	
Passive Sentences	100%
Flesch Reading Ease	40.0
Flesch-Kincaid Grade Level	13.3

OK

Comparing the statistics to the Reading Ease Scale, you can see that this sentence is far beyond the reading ease of most readers. And based on the grade-level scale, the text scored 13.3, or at college level.

By reducing the number of words and the sentence length, the readability statistics for this string are reduced.

"This wizard helps you select how Adobe Reader interacts with assistive technology."

Readability Statistics	?	✕

Counts	
Words	12
Characters	71
Paragraphs	1
Sentences	1
Averages	
Sentences per Paragraph	1.0
Words per Sentence	12.0
Characters per Word	5.8
Readability	
Passive Sentences	0%
Flesch Reading Ease	32.5
Flesch-Kincaid Grade Level	11.7

OK

Although most journals written for the public aim their writing at an eighth-grade reading comprehension level, depending on your target audience, you can decide on the appropriate target reading level. Paying attention to the reading level of your text and matching it to the reading levels of your intended audience will help you create text that is easily scanned and understood.

SUMMARY

In this chapter, you learned about research methods for understanding how users read online. Eye-tracking and mouse-tracking research helps us understand how users read and process user interface text.

- Through heat maps and gaze plots we can understand the area on the page that first catches the user's attention (first glance), how long users gaze on a particular area (gaze duration), how users visually move through the user interface (visual direction), how users scan pages and read text (scan patterns), how users scan pages when searching for specific items (search patterns).
- Mouse click heat maps show the areas over which the user moved the mouse and the mouse clicks on the page.
- Research shows that most users move through the page in an F pattern. When creating your user interface text, keep in mind that users scan text, starting from the top left corner and moving down the page. If you have important text or options, make sure they appear within the hotspots on the page.
- Readability scales help evaluate the reading levels content and understand the complexity of our text. Matching the readability levels of your text to the expected reading levels of your most common users will result in a better information experience.

CHAPTER 7

Applying Usability Principles to Your Writing

INTRODUCTION

In the previous chapter you saw how users view online pages and how they scan content. Understanding how users read online will help create the right information for helping users interact with your application. This includes deciding what information users need and the best way to integrate that information into the interface.

This chapter describes how usability guidelines and best practices apply to writing the text that appears within the application. Examples are presented throughout this chapter. When looking at these examples, think about the guidelines. What guidelines were followed, or where did the writers slip up? And ask yourself: How can this page be improved?

UNDERSTANDING YOUR USERS' INFORMATION NEEDS

Being guided by usability design principles when you are building your information experience will help you design, build, and write the text users need to interact successfully with your application. Now that you understand the guiding principles of how users scan and read online, you are ready to move onto the next phase: understanding what kind of information the user needs. Before you can apply these principles, you should first understand the user attributes that influence their information needs and how users will interact with the application.

UNDERSTANDING USER ATTRIBUTES

User attributes are the qualities and characteristics of your users that impact the amount and type of information you will provide. Following are the questions you should ask yourself each time you design and write the text that will appear on a surface in the application.

What Is the Current Knowledge Level of the User?

If your application is targeted toward a well-defined, cohesive group, you may be able to make assumptions about their skill levels. For example, if you are writing for business software that will be used by a specific user group, you may be able to assume that key phrases commonly used in that business environment will be understood by your users. These are the concepts, phrases, and terms you should use in the text. In fact, if you don't use terminology matching the user knowledge levels and expectations, your application may lose credibility.

The knowledge levels for applications created for a general audience are harder to gauge. Embedding helpful text into the surfaces, as well as explanations of key terms and phrases, may be required for users to understand the requirements and tasks.

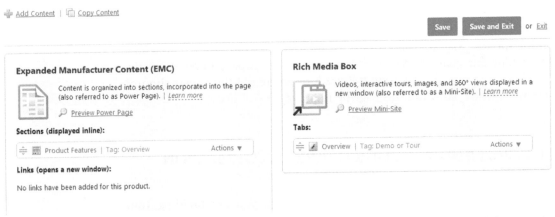

FIGURE 7.1 The key terms and phrases are defined to help users understand the concepts.

When in doubt, assume users are unfamiliar with professional terms and concepts and so provide the support they need to understand the interaction.

What Are the Users' Confidence and Motivation Levels?

Understanding confidence levels and motivational levels is not easily achieved. Are the users likely to enjoy the challenge, or will they be easily frustrated? Gamers, for example, are generally more comfortable trying to learn new ways of doing things, and will spend time playing around and experimenting with the application until they understand how it works.

Users who are less computer savvy are more easily frustrated. Trying to set up an online banking application or booking a vacation with several stops along the way may become stressful, and so these users will be less motivated to continue with the process. Using text to provide additional support may keep these users engaged, guiding them until they are successful. Adding callouts, help prompts, help links, and success messages to the user interface are ways you can provide support and encouragement to your users, while guiding them through the application.

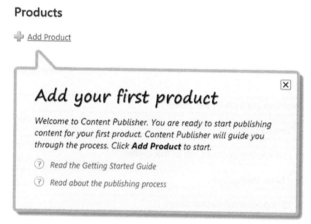

FIGURE 7.2 Help callouts can provide support and encouragement.

UNDERSTANDING INFORMATION ATTRIBUTES

Information attributes are all the elements and characteristics of your text that, when combined effectively, will make your user interface easy to read and useful for your users.

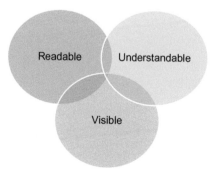

FIGURE 7.3 Information attributes.

Visibility

Even the best written text is not going to be very useful if the user can't find it. Users scanning the page should understand immediately which information is relevant for which controls. Information that is vital on a page should be easy to see and find.

Text Location

The placement of the text on the surface depends on where and when the user needs the piece of information. If a piece of information is crucial for making a selection, it should be easy to see, and should be directly next to, or above, the control to which it relates.

Although we know that users tend to scan a page from left to right, top to bottom, according to the Microsoft Windows Style Guide, users will most likely read the UI text in this order:

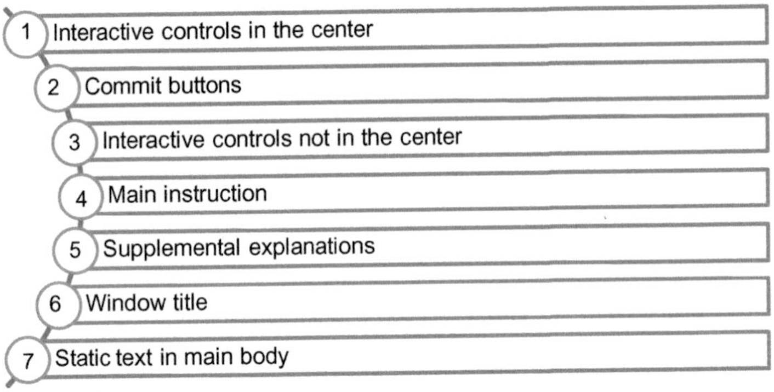

1 Interactive controls in the center
2 Commit buttons
3 Interactive controls not in the center
4 Main instruction
5 Supplemental explanations
6 Window title
7 Static text in main body

FIGURE 7.4 Reading order in the user interface (Microsoft Windows Style Guide).

The layout of this page makes it easy for users to understand the logic of the page, to find and read the relevant text, and to understand the interaction between the text, the options, and the commit buttons.

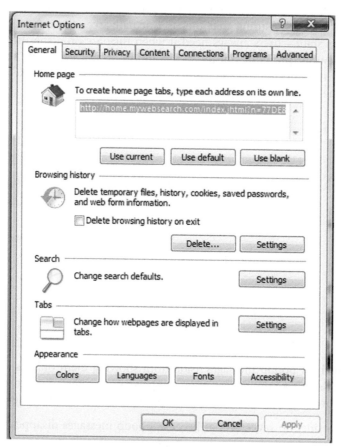

FIGURE 7.5 Example of a well-designed page.

One way to help users find information is to include the relevant text as part of the control itself. In this example, the information users need about restarting Outlook is part of the control. Users selecting this option are aware up front that they will need to restart the Outlook application.

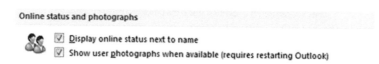

FIGURE 7.6 Placing important information directly in the control.

Popup Messages

If the user must know certain information before or after making a selection, or when moving between surfaces, you may decide that instead of placing the text directly on a surface, a popup message, or callout, is a better text medium. Popup messages, while they should be used sparingly, are often the best solution for ensuring that the user actually sees the information. If a message is static—users always need it when they are on a specific surface—then a popup is probably not the best solution. If, however, only some users will need the information, depending on the selection they make, a popup may be the right way to ensure the message is viewed.

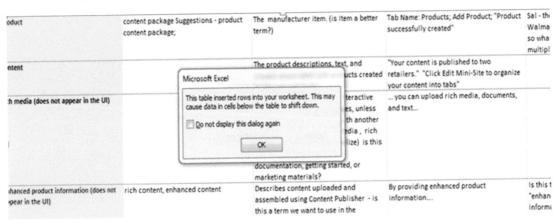

FIGURE 7.7 Example of a popup message.

One benefit of popup messages aside from showing them only as needed, is that they don't take up real estate on the page, nor do they distract users from focusing on other elements in the page, if and when the text is irrelevant.

One downside, however, is that because popup messages disappear after the user closes the message, any important information is no longer available after the user clicks OK or Cancel. For example, after closing the following message, users may not remember where they can view the update status. And once the information is gone, they have no way of recovering it.

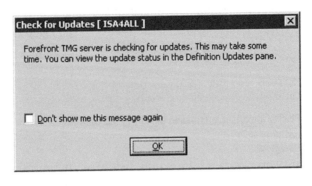

Readability

Readability refers to how easy it is to read your text. This sounds obvious and simple, but sometimes even the best written text comes out clumsy or too wordy when the message is placed on the surface. When writing for user interfaces, every effort should be made to provide text that is easy to scan and skim. Writing text that is concise and avoids extraneous information or information that is relevant in only a very few cases is one way to improve readability. Organizing your text into meaningful chunks, and deleting any extraneous words and punctuation, will also make it easier for users to interact with the page.

Conciseness

Concise text improves readability by keeping text to a minimum and eliminating any redundancy. Redundant text is either repetitive or not useful for completing the task at hand. Removing extraneous words or content improves the readability of your text by making it easier for users to find the information they need. Simple changes to your text can make a big difference in improving conciseness.

Extraneous Words…	Better
In order to add a picture to your album, select the Add Picture button.	To add a picture to your album, click Add Picture.
Select whether or not you want updates to be downloaded automatically.	Select if updates are downloaded automatically.

In your attempt to keep text concise and minimalistic, however, you should remember that users do need some guidance; therefore, removing all helpful text is not the goal.

Your text should be user focused and provide enough information for the user to understand the logic of the page, as well as the expected interaction. Conciseness alone does not make text more easily understood. As you can see in this example, some additional text would help the user understand the controls and options. The cryptic labels are not user-focused, and the layout of the page does not provide logical ordering of options, making it difficult to scan the page. Poor spacing and lack of alignment make it difficult to see the relationship between options.

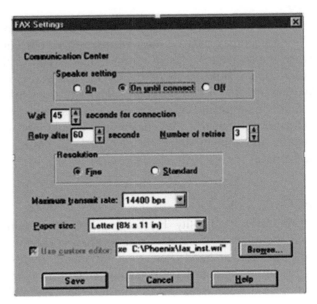

FIGURE 7.8 Example of overconcise text and poor layout.

Spacing

When you design and create your text, the spacing on the page should make it obvious which text and controls are related. White space between sections, group boxes, and proper alignment all provide visual cues, showing the connection between the elements on the page.

In this example, the developer tried to space everything out to balance the page. However, the end result is that it's difficult to discern which buttons actually belong with what text.

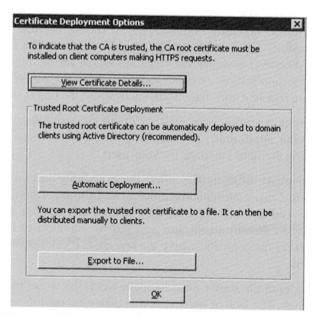

FIGURE 7.9 Example of incorrect spacing.

Here you can see how slight changes to the spacing improve the readability of the controls.

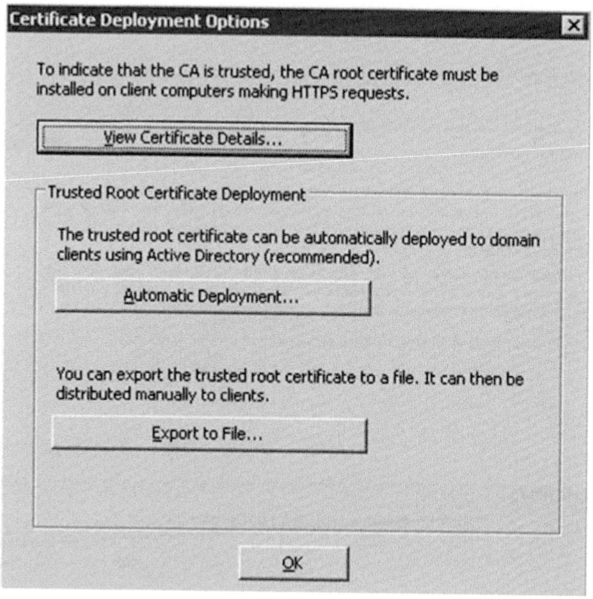

FIGURE 7.10 Improved spacing.

Understandability

For information to be easily understood, you should use the clearest, simplest text possible. The words you use depend on the target users of your application. Whenever possible, use common words and terminology associated with that application. When creating labels and object names, use names that are concrete and that effectively describe the object or action.

Learn the common terminology associated with the technology and features included in your application. This will help you communicate the concepts and ideas using the right language for your users.

Syntax and sentence structure also affect the readability and understandability of your text. Consistent sentence structure and shorter sentences are generally easier to read and understand. Also, making sure the key concepts and terms are easy to identify in the text and paying attention to how the sentence displays on the page and where the sentences break helps the readability of your text.

The following example shows what happens when the writer tries to overexplain the feature. The lack of spacing in this dialog makes the text difficult to comprehend, and there is a general lack of cohesiveness The explanation in the second paragraph may have been added for legal reasons, but it may have been better placed under the options as a warning or an informational note.

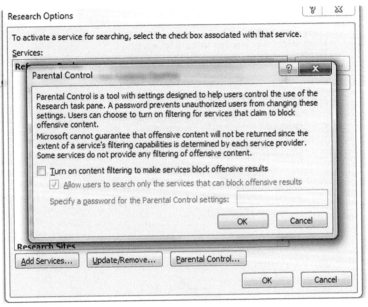

FIGURE 7.11 Example of too much text and poor organization.

Even a well-composed, concise sentence does not assure that text is easily understood. In this next example, the writer has good intentions. The sentence is concise and easy to read. However, the explanation is somewhat confusing and doesn't help the user decide which option to select.

FIGURE 7.12 Warning message sample.

The following text, provided in the help topic (opened by clicking the "Learn more" link), gives a far better explanation and could have been used in the dialog instead of the current text.

Accuracy

Even more important than conciseness and readability is the accuracy of your text. Users need to be certain that your text is correct in order to believe that it's worthwhile. If you're presenting technical information, be sure it has been reviewed by a subject matter expert. Providing sensible examples and logical recommendations improves the accuracy and overall trustworthiness of your content.

Accuracy is especially important in business and networking software where a simple mistake owing to unclear or inaccurate text can cost a company both time and money. And keep in mind that if network administrators in particular don't feel that they can trust the information in the user interface, they will not want to use your product.

With regard to consumer products, inaccurate text may not have a direct cost, but it will result in user frustration and a lack of confidence in your application. Once the trust is lost, users are hesitant to try the application again.

Consistency

Consistency refers to several aspects of your text—terminology, syntax, and text position. One of the simplest ways you can help readers scan your text is to provide consistent terminology, syntax, and text positioning.

Even a small glitch in consistency can cause confusion. In the following example, the inconsistent wording between the instruction in the block of text (*Change* password) and the button it relates to (*Create* password) can result in confusion. And although the user will probably figure out which button to click, it creates a poor impression and causes the user to pause unnecessarily.

FIGURE 7.13 Example of inconsistency within a surface.

Consistent Terminology

There are two types of terms you should pay attention to when creating text: terms you use when describing components of your user interface, and terms relating to the technologies and features in your application.

Terms describing the interface refer to the elements users interact with to complete their tasks (e.g., panels, windows, toolbars, task panes, button, and labels). Terms describing the technologies and features are directly related to the tasks and goals of the application. When describing the technologies and features, it's important to use the terms consistently, making it easier for users to scan the text to find key terms. Creating a terminology list for the team will help you define the correct terms and use them consistently across features and within other written materials. If, for example, your application requires users to configure a network adapter, you should decide whether to call it a network adapter, network interface card, or NIC. Then use the term consistently throughout the application.

Consistent Syntax

There are many different ways you can write a sentence or a phrase. Creating a style guide outlining how specific types of phrases or instructions are written will help your users and will ultimately save you time when writing the text. For example, if you have a list of system alerts or events, using a consistent style to write the alert name and description will help users scroll through them, finding the information they are seeking. If you have a landing page with a list of options, using the same format for each option will help users scan the list.

In this next example, you can see that each main section is a noun phrase as a title and that the options all begin with verbs. This helps users scan the page and find the options they need.

FIGURE 7.14 Example of consistent syntax.

Consistency is also important when users move between pages; using consistent language between surfaces helps users understand what is expected. In the following example, the instructions in the first page (on the left) do not match what the user sees in the next surface in the dialog (on the right) creating a confusing transition.

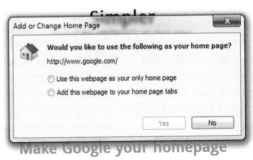

Understanding Task Attributes

Throughout the life cycle of an application, users perform a variety of tasks. The amount of textual support you provide and the depth of the text depend on the task itself. You will need to consider several attributes of each task before creating the accompanying user interface text. These attributes are task complexity, frequency, and learnability.

Complexity

Task complexity does not necessarily relate to the difficulty of the task; novice and advanced users alike often deal with complex tasks. Tasks are complex if they require several steps, or a sequence of steps to complete.

When planning the content for a complex task, it is helpful to ask yourself these questions:

- Is it clear how one step leads to another?
- Are there dependencies between options (steps)?
- At what point in the process will users require the most assistance?

After thinking about these questions, you can decide the best location for the text and how to break the text up into helpful chunks of information.

Task Frequency

Many tasks, such as setting up an account and installing a printer, are done once, or infrequently, throughout the product life cycle. Other tasks, such as logging into an application, adding an item, or generating a report, may be performed on a regular basis.

When designing your text, ask yourself:

- How frequently does the user need to complete this task?
- Is the task core to the application?

If a task is completed only once but is pivotal to the success of using the application, then it may require special instruction built into the workflow surface. Infrequent but complex tasks may benefit from creating a wizard to walk the user through the steps.

For example, in the following page, in order to complete the task, the user must enter the interest rate. The callout pointing to the field draws the user's attention to the task and also provides information on how to complete the field. The task on the right of the field lets the user know where he or she can look for the information. This is a good example of how you can help users complete an infrequent task that is key to completing a core task.

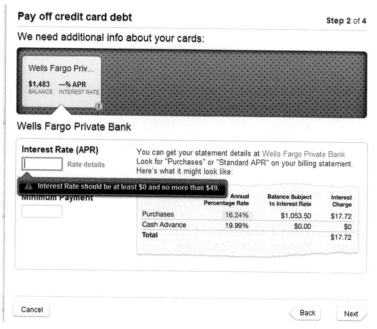

FIGURE 7.15 Helping users complete a core task (Mint.com).

Learnability

As in all tasks you complete throughout the day, some tasks are easy to learn, while others may have a steeper learning curve. When you create your information, think about the difficulty level of the task and the likelihood users will stumble through the steps each time they complete the task. Depending on the complexity of the task, the frequency, and the learning curve, you can decide the best approach for providing information. Wizards and integrated help balloons are good strategies for tasks with a high learning curve. If a task has a short learning curve, a simple text prompt and accurate label may be all that is required.

In this next example, first-time users will have a difficult time understanding how to get started using the tool.

FIGURE 7.16 A help prompt would help users get over the learning curve.

A simple help balloon or text prompt on the page would be valuable for helping users get started.

General Writing Considerations
Write about Tasks, Not Features

Software teams often think and plan in terms that describe product features and options. And since we talk about the application in these terms, it's easy to write in these terms as well. Before preparing your information, think about each task and what the user is trying to accomplish. Remember that users don't think about features, but rather think about actions.

Feature based – "I want to…"	Task based – "I want to…"
Run the Add Content Wizard	Add content to the page
Enable the caching checkbox	Cache content retrieved from the Internet
Define album properties	Design the pages of my album
Turn on track changes	Keep track of the changes I am making

Keeping the task in mind will help you write introductory text and labels that describe tasks and actions rather than the user interface—and avoid stating the obvious. In the first example below, the introductory text is almost a repetition of the checkbox text.

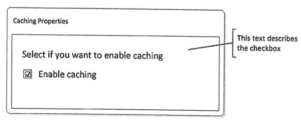

FIGURE 7.17 Example of feature-based text.

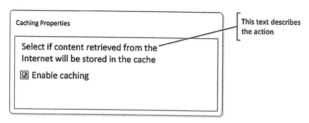

FIGURE 7.18 Example of task-based text.

In this example, little text is devoted to describing accessibility-related options and assistive technology; most of the information relates to how the wizard works rather than to the available options. And while the tone of the text is friendly, the content does not relate to the actions the user may want to take in the page.

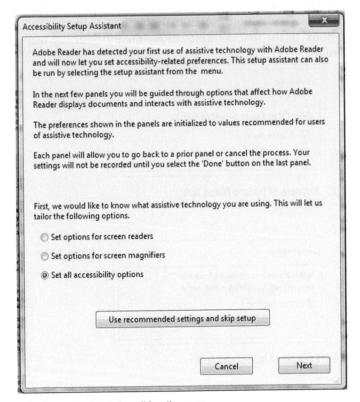

FIGURE 7.19 Example of text describing the page.

The following page provides another example of a textbox in which text placement, conciseness, and spacing should be improved. The nondescriptive frame titles don't provide helpful information. And the placement of the explanatory text is somewhat confusing; it isn't entirely clear from the block of text what will be ignored—the checkbox and the frequency setting, or both. If the text only relates to the second control, it should be placed next to that control.

FIGURE 7.20 Example of layout and text issues.

Provide Examples

One of the most effective and easiest ways to help users enter data and make selections in a page is to provide an example of the expected input. Examples can be far more effective than written descriptions or help topics.

In this example, not only is the description difficult to understand, but the input box does not provide the right visual clue as to how many digits are allowed.

ACCOUNT PIN & SECRET QUESTION

Your Account PIN is Really Important

You'll need your Account PIN to add money, login and purchase items from the downloads store. Please write down your Account PIN and keep it somewhere safe. It must be 6 numbers long (no letters or special characters). No more than 3 identical numbers in a row (222). No more than 3 sequential numbers (234).

Create Your Account PIN (vKey)*

`••••••••`

Confirm Your Account Pin (vKey)*

`••••••••`

After entering a PIN incorrectly, this is the error provided.

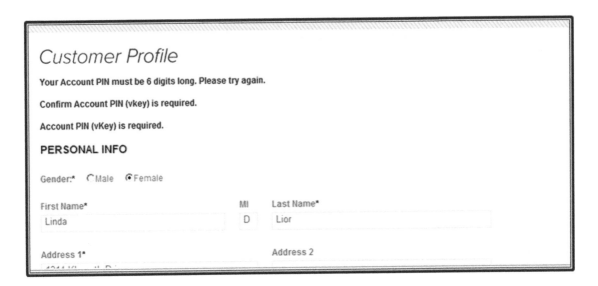

Adding an example with a sample PIN number under the input box would provide the crucial information that the PIN must be exactly six digits long, and at the same time demonstrate the constraints of the PIN in a way that is much easier for the user to understand. Also, moving the text describing the PIN so that it is easier to read would help users understand the PIN requirements.

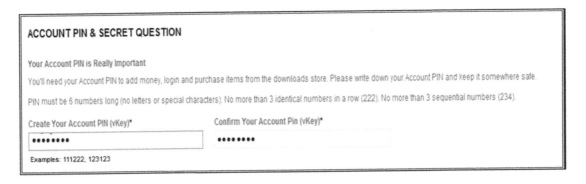

Examples can take on many different forms, depending on what the user must enter, helping users understand what data they are searching for, or what values to enter. Examples are particularly helpful when users must enter a string, such as a URL that must be written in a specific format.

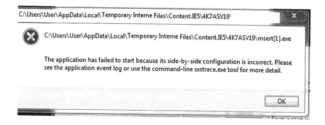

FIGURE 7.21 Add examples to clarify input format.

In the input box, adding an example would help users understand the format that should be used (e.g., https://www.mysite.com).

Using the Right Language

Previous chapters discussed ways to learn about your users and different types of users. When creating your messages, keep in mind the target users and use language that is appropriate for that group.

This error message may be appropriate for an IT administrator, but the computer jargon and recommended actions (sending the user to the event log or to the command-line) are far too technical for a home user.

On the other end of the spectrum, web applications in particular use informal language and tone. Keep in mind that while your tone should be friendly, it should also be appropriate for the application and user. For example, in the following screen, this text "yada yada" is fine for Google, but would be inappropriate for a business software application. While Google is able to get away with this kind of informality, it's somewhat doubtful that users will understand the terms *latency* and *site latency* used in the explanatory text.

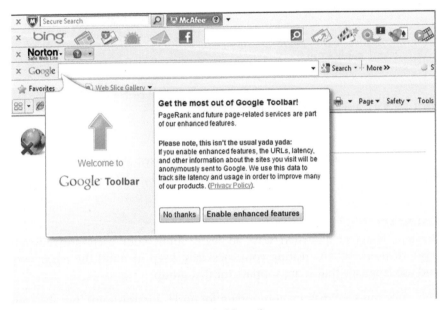

FIGURE 7.22 Use the right terms and level of formality.

General Text Usability Guidelines

In the earlier sections, we talked how to improve the information experience for your users. Below is a list of the general guidelines for you to refer to when creating and writing the information appearing in the user interface.

1. Use natural language, choosing terms, keywords, phrases, and concepts that are familiar to users. Avoid the tendency to use computer jargon when common, easier to understand words are available.
2. Use consistent terminology, consistent syntax, and consistent style throughout the application. This will help users find the keywords and phrases.
3. Avoid words such as "terminate" and "abort" that have a negative connotation, when a better word is available—for example, "end" or "stop," respectively.
4. Always use a tone that is user-focused, encouraging, and positive. Never blame the user or make the user feel inadequate by using condescending or angry language. The tone should be friendly and straightforward. Avoid any legal or corporate undertones. And never use a sarcastic tone.
5. Let users know how they are proceeding. The outcome of an action should be obvious, with feedback provided to let users know that they are moving along successfully, that the system is processing the action, or that an error has occurred.

6. If an error or warning message is required, the message should include a brief explanation of what caused the incident and should provide ways to amend the problem and continue.
7. Avoid using technical terms and system code in the message, and don't suggest a fix that requires technical knowledge beyond the user's capabilities.
8. Text should be accurate and relevant for the current page or task. Adding nice-to-know information will slow the user down and may even cause confusion.
9. Your text should guide users toward their goals. If additional information beyond what you can offer in the interface is required, consider adding help callouts or help prompts to the surface.
10. Text and options that go together should be spaced near each other so that the relationship between the text and associated controls is visually apparent.
11. Help links within the interface should navigate to a topic relevant to the task users are focused on when clicking the link; it should not take users to a general help page or landing page.

WHAT ARE THE KEY COMPONENTS OF A POSITIVE INFORMATION EXPERIENCE?

Saul Carliner, PhD, CTDP

Editor-in-Chief, IEEE Transactions on Professional Communication

Ultimately, the goal of a positive information experience is to have users find the information they need and perform the task of interest as quickly as possible—and succeed on the first try.

This sounds easy, but getting there is hard work. First, we need to make sure that users find the information needed quickly. That requires a good information architecture and clear navigation, as well as a good search capability.

When users find the information they want, we need to make sure that the information is really the information sought (sometimes, it merely appears that way). To do so, we need to identify areas of possible confusion and put pointers both in the search systems and, at the top of pages that might be confused, to help users figure out quickly whether or not they're really where they want to be.

If they're there, we need to think about the user experience at that moment and address expectations (either directly or acknowledge that we're not going to do so). Genre theory is the most helpful framework for this because genres, at their core, are about the unwritten expectations that users bring to well-defined situations. We need to correctly identify the "genre" we're dealing with, take time to identify the expectations users have with that genre (most of which are never formally documented), and then make an effort to address them.

Of course, communicating in plain language and presenting information that's accurate and instructions that really work are essential. And definitely provide visuals if they're going to help clarify the written content.

But sometimes that doesn't happen for reasons beyond our control. So we also need to provide a means for helping users acknowledge whether or not the information met their needs and, if not, help lead them to the correct information (to the best of our ability to anticipate likely errors).

In other words, the components of a positive information experience start with thinking about what a user might want at a particular moment, how users might think and respond, and designing and writing accordingly.

SUMMARY

In this chapter, you learned how users read and process user interface text. Remembering these principles will help you create content that helps your users read and understand how to interact with your application.

- When creating your user interface text, keep in mind that users scan text, starting from the top left corner and moving down the page. If you have important text or options, make sure they appear within the hotspots on the page.
- When writing your text, think about user attributes, information attributes, and task attributes.
- When designing your information, consider the complexity, frequency, and learnability of a task.
- Examples are an effective way to help users enter data and make selections on a page.
- Your text should focus on the tasks users want to complete, not on the features.
- Following the usability guidelines for text will help you create text that is easy to scan and understand.

CHAPTER 8

Creating Writing Guidelines

INTRODUCTION

Before you begin writing your text, it's a good idea to define the writing guidelines you will use and to come up with a clear set of guidelines for your user interface text. The guidelines will become a valuable source of information for the developers, product managers, and technical writers. It will also help you create a user interface that is consistent across features and products.

In addition, your application should meet the guidelines for accessibility and globalization. Creating and understanding these guidelines will help you create text that is easily navigated and easily localized.

This chapter describes the elements that go into creating a style guide and the guidelines for building accessibility into your user interface text. It also describes ways to make your application easily localized and read for an international audience.

WHAT IS A STYLE GUIDE?

A style guide is a practical document describing the standards for writing and designing information for a company, product line, or application. A company may have several different style guides—one for internal documents, customer facing documents, product documentation, online help topics, and user interface text. While creating a style guide may take some time upfront, there are many benefits that ultimately result in uniform, easy to read content within the application.

Each application has a variety of surfaces and content types. Defining the format and writing styles for each surface and element in your user interface will ultimately save you time trying to decide where and how to present information on each page.

Using a style guide is especially useful when you have more than one writer on a project, or if writers are replaced during a project. A style guide helps keep the text consistent between writers, and if you have several developers and product managers, each writing his or her own text, it will help keep the text consistent across the application. When a user moves through the user interface, consistency across an application helps the reader stay oriented and on task—and less distracted by changes from page to page.

When creating your style guide, it's also a good idea to remember that many large companies, including Apple, have style guidelines available to the public. If your product runs on one of these operating systems, you may find it useful to integrate and use many of the styles and writing rules they recommend. While you will still need to create guidelines specific to your own application, looking at existing style recommendations can save you time when preparing your own style guide.

The main purpose of a style guide is to ensure your text is easy to read and understand.

What Does A Style Guide Include?

A style guide should include your team's standards for writing text as well as directions on how and where text should be placed on each surface.

A good style guide will let the team know the fonts that should be used, how the text is placed on the page, and the way text is written (e.g., language, tone, vocabulary). It should also include details about adhering to accessibility guidelines and considerations for localizing and globalizing your application.

When creating your style guide, consider creating guidelines for each of these main topics:

- Writing style
- Typography guidelines
- Writing guidelines for each content type

DEFINING WRITING STYLE GUIDELINES

Writing style guidelines define how text should be written; your writing style should make it easier for users to understand and interact with the controls and options presented in the interface. When defining your writing style and guidelines, such as punctuation, it's a good idea to use a known source as your "go to" guide. *The Chicago Manual of Style* is well known in the technical writing world as a leading source of information about punctuation and writing style guidelines. *The Microsoft Manual of Style for Technical Publications* provides many good examples of writing guidelines for user–computer interaction.

Writing style is a combination of factors—such as tone, and language, and sentence structure.

Writing Style

Deciding on the Appropriate Tone

When having a conversation, your tone changes depending on the person you are speaking to and the context of the conversation. In a single conversation, your tone may change several times: You may start out formally and move to an informal tone, fluctuating between humorous and serious, or from light-hearted to angry and back again. When writing user interface text, the options for tone are somewhat limited to informative, friendly, and supportive, generally all at the same time.

While the level of formality remains constant throughout the application, some changes in tone are appropriate, and occasionally some humor may be useful for making your users feel more comfortable. Remember, however, that humor, if resorted to at all, should be used sparingly and only under the right conditions.

Tone is created by the words you choose and your style of writing.

For example, the following message uses an informal tone, with some humor. Notice that the message does not place any blame on the user for opening a web page or tab that caused the problem. It lets the user know in a friendly way that there is a problem, and it gives possible reasons for the problem as well as possible ways to remedy the situation.

FIGURE 8.1 Example of informal tone.

Choosing the Right Language

Although tone is a function of the way you write, language is about choosing the right words and how you put words together.

The language and terminology you use should take into account your users' knowledge, skills, and other relevant demographics, such as education, age, and gender. If your company already has marketing and sales publications, you may need to align your text with the marketing and business messages of the company. At the same time, you need to remember that user interface text should be concise avoiding marketing buzz words and other corporate language. Keeping in mind the personas for your application will also help you choose the right words for your messages.

Here are some guidelines to follow, along with any guidelines specific to your industry, company, and application.

- *Use common language but avoid slang.* Common language is easy to understand and easy to translate. This is everyday language, as if you are having a conversation with the user. And while some slang may be well known to many of your users, it may be difficult for nonnative English speakers to understand. Moreover, some slang words are understood differently by different age groups and may be considered too informal by some users.
- *Use terminology users will understand.* Use the standard industry terms if they exist and are commonly used. If there is a common term that your users will understand, then that is the word you should use. If, however, your users won't understand the industry term, then explain it in words they will understand. For example, if your users are IT professionals, they will of course understand the difference between an HTTP and HTTPS connection. If they are not IT professionals or are working in a network-related environment, you will need to explain the difference.
- *Use acronyms when the acronym is better known than the full term.* When an acronym has become the common way of relating to an object or a concept, then you should use that acronym in the user interface. Not only will it save space, but it will make the text easier to comprehend. For example, users may have a more difficult time understanding "Internet protocol address" than the more commonly used term "IP address." Writing "Digital Versatile/Video Disc" instead of DVD would similarly confuse users.
- *Avoid long words when a shorter word for the same thing exists.* If a shorter word can be just as precise and easily understood, then use it. For example, photo instead of photograph, e-mail or email instead of electronic mail.
- *If more than one term exists for an object, choose the term that best suits your users, and then use that term throughout.* For example, the terms *image*, *picture*, and *photo* are often used interchangeably. Select the most accurate and common term, and then use it exclusively.

Putting the Words Together

Using the right tone and language also includes making your users feel comfortable and putting them at ease. The way in which you write can make a big difference in how your users perceive your software, and whether or not they enjoy the interaction. Here are some simple rules to follow that will help you guide your users in a positive way:

- *Write in the positive.* When you think about someone you enjoy speaking with or listening to, most likely their speech patterns encompass positive thoughts, words, and gestures. Your users will also appreciate a positive, supportive tone. The user interface is not the place to scold, blame, or use negative or condescending language.

- *Be the authority, but avoid being authoritative.* The information you provide should be accurate but you should not talk down to your users. Avoid writing as if you are the computer, and also avoid using corporate jargon. The words you use and your style of writing should elicit a positive reaction from your users.

- *Explain new concepts but avoid overexplaining.* Introducing a new idea or concept can be difficult in the user interface. On one hand, you want users to have enough information to understand what they are doing and to make logical selections. On the other hand, the user interface is not ideal for teaching concepts and large blocks of text. If your application supports help links, you can provide just enough information for users to understand the options on the page. Then, provide more information using a help link— either opening a help balloon in the page or navigating to a help topic.

- *Remember that the user is a person, not an object.* Messages should be directed toward the person sitting at the computer, using the application. Also remember to address the user as "you" when it's appropriate.

- In this example, the user may be somewhat taken aback by being the focus of the message *"You are not fully protected."* A better, more accurate message would be *"Your computer is not fully protected."*

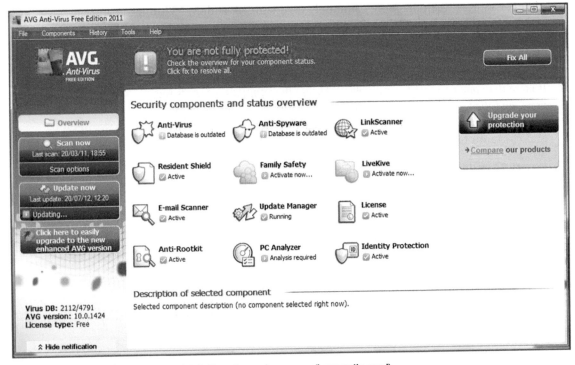

FIGURE 8.2 User-focused message (incorrectly used).

Punctuation

Punctuation can help speed up reading by clarifying the meaning of your sentences. Your guidelines should cover the types of punctuation that are acceptable and not acceptable. When it comes to user interface text, shorter sentences are generally easier to read.

Common punctuation marks you should specify in your guidelines are presented in the following table together with some sample guidelines. You may want to add more examples and guidelines for your application.

Punctuation mark	Example guidelines
Comma ,	Use a comma in a series of more than two sequential items. A, B, and C Use commas according to *The Chicago Manual of Style*
Colon :	Avoid colons except at the end of a command or when showing an example. Example: Enter the name of the computer:
Semicolon ;	Semicolons create long, complex sentences and should be avoided in user interface text
Question mark ?	Use question marks when the user action is directly related to a question. Do you want to continue? How do you want to configure this computer?
Period .	Use a period at the end of a complete sentence.
Exclamation mark !	Do not use exclamation marks in the user interface text. Instead, use the caution icon at the beginning of a sentence.
Ellipsis …	Use the ellipsis to indicate that more information or another option will follow.
Dash —	Use dashes (em dash) only when needed to set off an explanation, example, or comment from the main thought of a sentence. Do not use a dash to hyphenate words.
Parentheses ( )	Use parentheses only as needed. Put a period inside the parentheses if it is a complete sentence.
Slash /	Use the slash as needed to indicate a path. Do not use and/or.
Plural "s" Avoid using (s) or /s to indicate a possible plural	Avoid using this construct. If possible, write in the plural form unless the value will always be singular. Correct: Select the pictures for this album: Wrong: Select the picture or pictures for this album: Wrong: Select the picture(s) for this album: Wrong: Select the picture/s for this album:

TYPOGRAPHY GUIDELINES

At the most basic level, typography refers to the typefaces and fonts used for displaying the text in your application. Typefaces are a family of fonts, such as Ariel, Helvetica, and Segoe. When you select a font, you also define the size of your letters. Each family of fonts may have several associated fonts (i.e., styles) within that family (as shown in the following table).

Examples of Typefaces (Font Family)	Examples of font styles
Helvetica	**Helvetica Bold** *Helvetica Italic*
Ariel	**Ariel Bold** Ariel Black *Ariel Italic* Ariel Rounded Bold
Segoe	Segoe UI Semi Bold Segoe Print Segoe UI

Typography affects the legibility and readability of your text and strongly impacts the reading speed and comfort of users.

- **Legibility** is the ease with which the reader can distinguish one letter from another. In general, legible typefaces usually have larger closed or open inner spaces.
- **Readability**, as mentioned in previous chapters, refers to how well and how easily text delivers its message to a reader of that text. While reader ability, motivation, and knowledge, as well as vocabulary and text structure, affect readability, typology—typeface, font size, text spacing, and layout—affect the overall readability of your text.

If you have UX designers or graphic artists working on your application, they are usually highly involved in defining the fonts and styles used within the interface. They have been trained to understand how users react to colors and different fonts, and they can create the typography guidelines for you. In the absence of a designer, look at applications you find easy to read and scan and use similar fonts and styles.

Here are some typography guidelines for making your text more legible and readable:

- Create a typography hierarchy that defines fonts for headings, body text, options, links, notes, and the like. A consistent typography hierarchy helps users understand the structure of your content and helps them read through the page.

- Define the typeface that will be used. Typefaces are either serif or sans serif. A serif font includes the small turns that finish the strokes of letters in a font; sans serif font doesn't include the small finishing strokes. Serif fonts (such as Times New Roman) are generally used in print materials. For UI texts, the need for a clean appearance and the lower resolution of computer monitors impacts which fonts to use; sans serif typefaces are considered easier to read online.

- Specify text and background colors. Using high-contrasting colors easily distinguishes the font color and background color. In general, black text on a white background is the easiest for users to read. Low contrasting colors, such as a blue on a black background causes eye fatigue, as does reading bright colors on a bright background (e.g., yellow text on green). There are two major types of colorblindness: difficulty in distinguishing between red and green, and difficulty in distinguishing between blue and yellow. Avoid colors and color combinations that are difficult for colorblind people to distinguish. Use color text sparingly, if at all. Remember that text alone should never be used to call out important information.

- Improve the scanability of your pages by defining consistent and appropriate letter spacing, alignment, and line height. This includes spacing between the lines of text, as well as between the text and the top, sides, and bottom margins of the page.

- Define the optimal line length (the number of words per line). The user should be able to easily scan a line of text. Long lines are difficult to visually track, making it difficult for users to find their way to the next line. Lines that are too short often have so many line breaks that they are also difficult to read. In general, each line should be somewhere between 45 and 75 characters long (66 characters is often cited as ideal).

- Define when and how bold text is appropriate. In general, use bold text sparingly and only to emphasis a particular option or important word. Bold text draws the eye toward it; when too many words are boldface, the boldface text loses its impact.

In the following example, you can see how bold is used to draw the user's attention to the current status of the system. This is a good example of how bold can be useful when used sparingly.

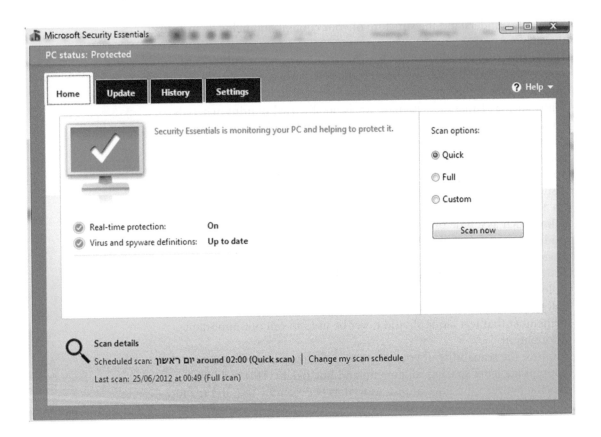

- Define rules for hyphenation and how lines should break between words. There may be words that you always want kept together (i.e., require a nonbreak space between them). This would include product and feature names or special terms and concepts. Include these words in your style guide with specific rules on how to use them.
- Define guidelines for blinking or otherwise animated text. Blinking and moving text is difficult to read and highly distracting. Unless you have a specific reason for using moving text, it's best to avoid it altogether.

Good typography reduces the effort required by the user to read and understand the text.

DEFINING GUIDELINES FOR EACH CONTENT TYPE

Your style guide should present writing guidelines for each content type and surface included in your user interface. This will help you write more efficiently and provide a more consistent user experience. The sections below describe surfaces found in typical applications, and general guidelines for writing user interface text for these surfaces.

Landing Pages

In web site design, a landing page is a web page that provides additional information after a user clicks on a link from another web page or clicks on an embedded advertisement. In a web or software application, a landing page is usually the first page a user sees when logging into the application. It generally provides information about the application and links to main options and features. An application may have multiple landing pages, one for each main task or node in the application.

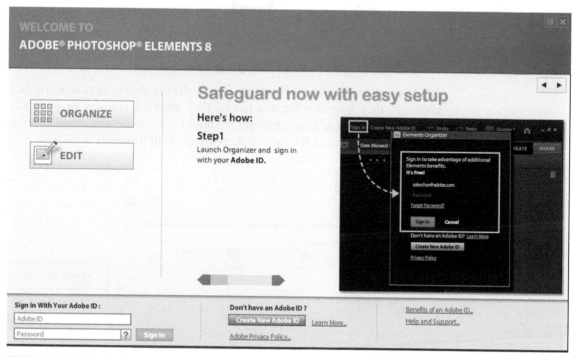

FIGURE 8.3 Example of a main landing page.

FIGURE 8.4 Example of a feature landing page.

While the two examples of landing pages, shown above, appear to be very different, they have similar text needs. Each element requires its own font and style of writing. Your style guide should include details about the formatting and style used for each of these types of information.

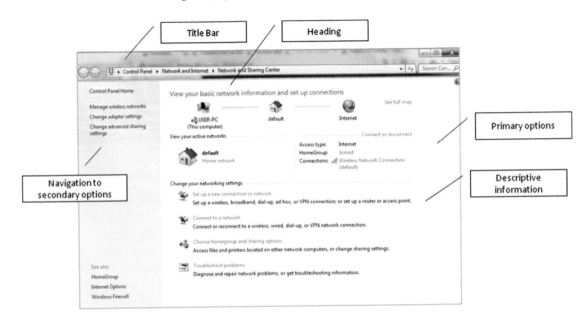

Text Element	Purpose
Title bar	Located at the top of the page, the title usually provides the name of the application, node, or feature, depending on where it's located in the application. When you think about guidelines for a title bar, you will want to decide on capitalization, the structure of the title, and the syntax that you will use.
Heading	The heading lets the user know the purpose of the page. It can be written as a noun phrase or as an instruction. While consistency is important, you may find that some pages are more suited for headings written as commands, others may require noun phrases, and some may be questions.
Primary options	The primary options are generally located in the main section or pane of the page. Whether the options are buttons or hyperlinks, the text should describe the task the user will launch when the option is selected.
Descriptive information	Text within the page provides additional information about the available options.
Secondary options or features	The buttons and links within the panels allow users to navigate to different options within the application.
Links to help	Links are often provided as "Learn more" or as hyperlink with the name of the help topic. Help links within the application should lead users to a specific topic in the help center.

Notice in all three landing page examples above, that the tone is informal and friendly, and that the options are written for taking action—starting with an action word (launch, set up, choose, connect, etc.), while labels are nouns or noun phrases (e.g., home network).

Wizards

Wizards help users when they have to complete a series of steps that must be completed sequentially. They are also good for complex tasks where users have a better chance of getting through the tasks successfully with the additional guidance and support a wizard provides.

Traditionally, wizard pages had a similar look and feel, with standard phrasing and formatting, like the samples below.

(a)   (b)

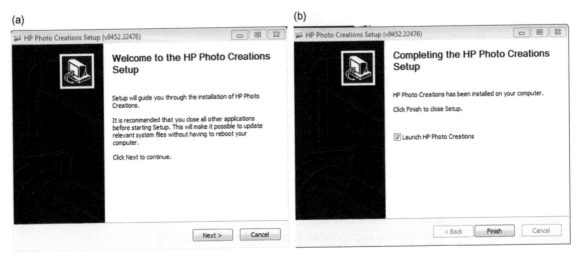

FIGURE 8.5 Traditional look of software wizard pages.

In current years, with more applications developed for the web, wizards now come in many variations with friendlier graphics and visuals, as well as various navigation options, such as a navigation pane.

Wizards generally have three types of pages: a welcome page, interior pages, and a completion page.

- The *welcome page* provides a short introduction, giving the users an overview of what tasks they will accomplish by running the wizard. Welcome pages should be written in a way that makes it easy for the users to scan the text. Using consistent phrasing for all your welcome pages will help users scan the page and find the important information.
- *Interior pages* provide the settings and options the users interact with to complete the wizard. The text you create for these pages should guide the users, helping them make the right selections and successfully complete the wizard. In some cases, inner pages may also be used to provide important information and may not have any settings in the page.
- The *completion page* provides a summary of the settings that will be applied when the users click the button to finish the wizard. Similar to welcome pages, you should design the text for scanning, making it easy for users to find the relevant information.

Your style guide should include standard phasing for welcome pages and the completion page, as well as for the elements appearing across the interior pages.

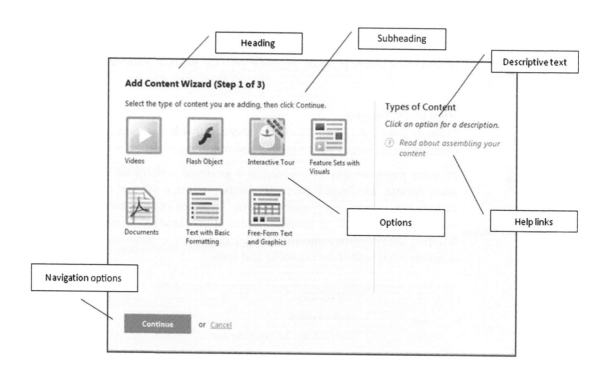

Your guidelines for wizard pages should include text formatting, writing styles, and capitalization for these elements appearing in your wizard pages.

Text Element	Purpose
Title bar or heading	Provides the name of the wizard, such as Getting Started Wizard.
Subheading	Provides the main instruction or prompt.
Options	Provide the labels and text elements that are part of the widgets the users interact with.
Descriptive or informative texts	Provide information about the available options.
Navigation buttons or links	Are used to move between the wizard pages (e.g., Next, Back, Finish).
Help links	Are often provided as "Learn more" or as hyperlink with the name of the help topic. Help links lead users to a specific topic that will help the user make a selection in the page.

When writing your text guidelines for wizards, keep in mind that the labels are generally written as commands; they use active words such as Select, Choose, Pick, and Enter. Because wizards are often considered a form of help designed for novice users, advanced users usually prefer to skip wizards and use property pages instead. This gives them the flexibility to navigate freely between options. When creating your text guidelines, remember that it's important to use consistent terminology for corresponding settings, wherever they appear—whether in wizards, property pages, or even the documentation.

Property Pages

Property pages, also called property sheets, provide the various options and controls users interact with to select and modify application settings.

Property pages are often presented as a group of surfaces, all relating to the same feature. Traditional property sheets provide a tab for each page and include OK, Apply, and Cancel buttons. In recent years, there's been a shift in the look and feel of property sheets from standard windows forms to building the properties into the HTML page. Property pages now come in all different sizes, with differing looks and feels.

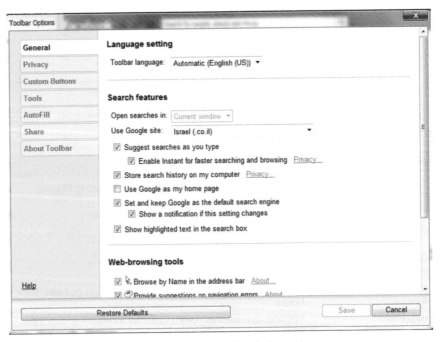

FIGURE 8.6 Example of web-based properties (Google Chrome).

Looking at the page in Figure 8.6, one it's difficult to tell the difference between the controls in this page and a wizard page. In a set of property pages, controls are related, but the configuration does not have to occur in a sequence and in many cases, users don't need to complete any tasks at all: They can rely on the default values.

Regardless of the style (standard form or HMTL), property sheets tend to have similar text elements.

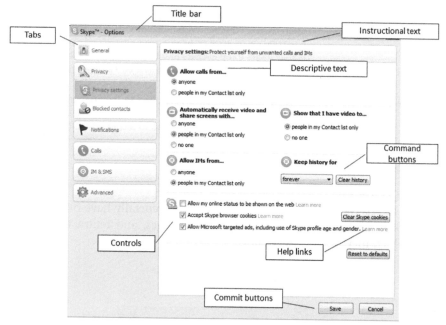

FIGURE 8.7 Example of text elements in an HTML-based property page.

Your guidelines for property pages should include text formatting, writing styles, and capitalization for these elements:

Text Element	Purpose
Title bar	The title bar provides a name for all the pages in the group. The text in the title should match the name of the menu item, button, or link from which the property pages are launched.
Tabs	The tab name provides a label for the group of controls in the specific page. Try to use concrete labels. Generic labels, such as Advanced, Preferences, or Options are not very helpful when users are searching for specific controls.
Instructive text (introductory text)	The instructive text describes the overall actions the user should take, or the purpose of the page.
Descriptive or informative texts	These texts describe and provide information about the available options.
Controls and options	These are the labels and text elements that are part of the widgets with which the users interact.
Group separators	A group separator is a short label separating one group of controls from another. In some instances a frame is used instead of a line.

Continued...

Continued	
Text Element	**Purpose**
Command buttons	Command buttons are used to initiate an action or to open related controls. When the command button opens a dialog box or another type of user interface element, the text includes three ellipses at the end (e.g., Settings…)
Commit buttons	Usually standard buttons are used (OK, Cancel, and Apply, or Save and Apply).
Help links	Links are often included in the page as "Learn more" or as hyperlinks with the name of the help topic. Help links within the application should lead users to a specific topic in the help center.

Dialog Boxes

Dialog boxes, in comparison to property sheets, generally have only one surface. Users configure the settings, save the changes, and return to the page from which they opened the dialog.

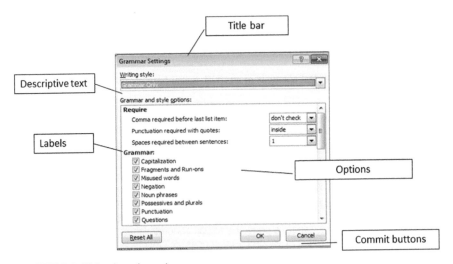

FIGURE 8.8 Dialog box elements.

Dialog boxes may contain a single option or a complete set of controls. While property pages and wizards tend to have standard sizes throughout an application, dialog boxes are often sized according to the number of controls and amount of information placed in the page.

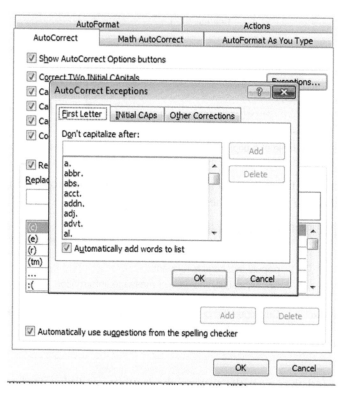

FIGURE 8.9 Example of a dialog opening from a property page.

Dialog boxes have the same text elements as property sheets, although they may not include all the elements, such as tabs. When writing your text guidelines for property pages and dialog boxes, keep in mind that users often view the options to understand how the application is configured but don't modify or select any settings. For example, in network applications, it's common practice for network administrators to complete the initial configuration and then review all the settings to understand the defaults and make minor modifications as needed. Text and labels on these surfaces are more descriptive and less instructive.

Your guidelines for dialog boxes should describe the standards for capitalization and general text guidelines for each element, as listed in the property page elements table.

Popup Messages

Popup messages display in response to an action made by either the user or the computer. Most popup messages have a similar style and contain the same basic elements.

FIGURE 8.10 Example of a popup message.

Your guidelines for popup messages should include text formatting, writing styles, and capitalization for these elements:

Text Element	Purpose
Title bar	Lets the user know the application, feature, or option for which the popup message is relevant.
Icon	Shows visually the type of message: information, warning, error, security, etc.
Descriptive text	Describes the purpose of the message and the possible actions the user can or should take.
Commit buttons	Provide the user selections.

Keep in mind that even the text on the buttons, or links, used to close or accept an action impact the user experience and should match the user's situation and expectation. If you ask a question, then the choices should provide possible answers to the question (e.g., Yes/No). If you provide two options, then it should be clear which button results in what action.

Popup messages often use icons to indicate the kind of message—informational, warning, security, or confirmation. Your team may have customized icons or may use the standard icons. Either way, it's important to use them consistently.

While popup message have the same general look, there are different types of messages, each with its own purpose and style. When you create your style guidelines, remember to keep in mind the different type of popup messages: validation, informative, confirmation, warning, and error messages.

Validation Messages

When the user is required the enter values or fill in forms, the application validates the information and provides feedback. Sometimes these messages are positive, telling the user that the action was successful. Other times, these messages are meant to let the user know that they have made an error that requires them to reenter information or fill in missing fields. While each validation message provides different content, your guidelines should specify the formatting for each element and provide generic samples for similar messages.

FIGURE 8.11 Example of a validation message.

Informative Messages

Sometimes a user action results in a change that may or may not have an expected outcome. When this happens, a message is often provided, letting the users know what to expect, or asking them if they want to continue with the action.

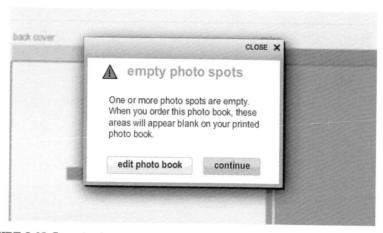

FIGURE 8.12 Example of an informative message.

Confirmation Messages

When it's important to make sure users understand what will happen when an action completes, confirmation messages are provided, offering the user the option to confirm or alter the action. While each confirmation message will be different, your guidelines can include the overall formatting of the text and can also provide generic messages that can be used wherever relevant.

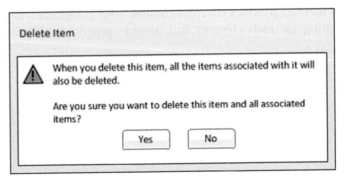

FIGURE 8.13 Example of a confirmation message.

Warning Messages

Warning messages let the user know when something unexpected may occur or has occurred. While your application may have different forms of warning messages, your guidelines should provide sample strings for the various warning messages in the system. Also make sure you specify the types of icons that should be used in conjunction with each type of message string and for what purpose.

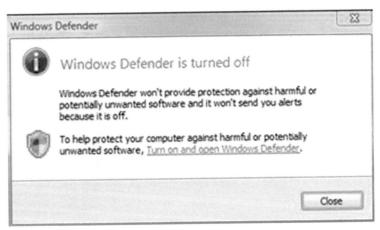

FIGURE 8.14 Example of a warning message for a security issue.

It's also a good idea to include the standards for commit buttons in warning and other popup messages. Forcing a user to click OK, as in the following example, can be frustrating.

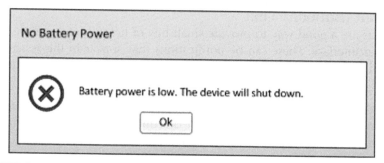

FIGURE 8.15 Sample of a warning message.

When writing popup messages, it's important to provide text that is friendly and supportive. Otherwise, users may become frustrated and annoyed by the additional steps or actions required of them. And remember that every word counts.

Error Messages

Error messages occur as a reaction to a user action or to an occurrence that the user did not explicitly initiate. Error messages, when well written, have the ability to help users through a situation. When written poorly, error messages are a source of frustration, and even anger.

Your style guidelines for error messages should include the layout, format, and syntax used for each type of error message. A good error message tells the user what happened and provides possible solutions to fix the issue. Your guidelines should provide samples showing how to write error messages with a supportive tone. The guidelines should also include the formatting for any help links included in the error message.

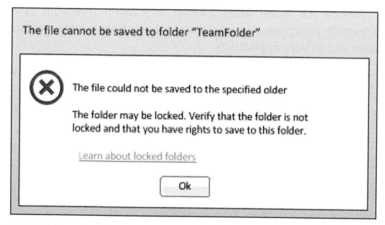

FIGURE 8.16 Example of an error message.

Callout (Balloon) Text

Callouts are a good way to provide small bits of helpful information within the user interface. These can be notifications that appear in the system tray, helpful hints integrated into the user interface, or validation messages displayed next to the relevant controls.

Each type of callout you add to your interface should have a consistent format and style. Your guidelines should describe punctuation, capitalization, and syntax for each type of element in the callouts.

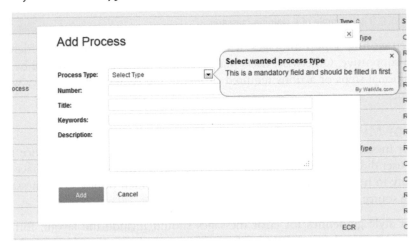

FIGURE 8.17 Example of a balloon callout.

Tooltips and Hover Text

Tooltips and hover text provide additional information about a graphical element or an available option. They are often used in toolbars and ribbon bars and to explain the menu items. Similar to balloon text, your guidelines should include punctuation, capitalization, and syntax for the various types of tooltips and in your application.

FIGURE 8.18 Example of a tooltip.

SUMMARY

Style guides help software teams create an information experience that is consistent between surfaces and features.

- A good style guide will include details about writing styles and typography.
- Creating a typography hierarchy that defines fonts for headings, body text, options, links, and all text elements will help improve the legibility and readability of your text.
- Writing style consists of tone, language (the words you choose), and syntax. A good style guide includes samples of these components.
- Your style guide should present writing guidelines for each content type and the elements comprising each content type.
- Your style guide should provide samples of strings. This is particularly useful for the different popup and error messages.

Creating Your Information Experience

The previous chapters in the book described the components that comprise the information experience and how to understand the information needs of your users. This section describes how you create the content users will rely on when they are interacting with your application.

This section also describes how to create content that meets the needs of diverse audiences and provides an information experience that crosses cultural boundaries.

CHAPTER 9

Designing Your Information Strategy

INTRODUCTION

After you understand the abilities, main tasks, and work practices of your users, you can plan the information experience design strategy. The strategy outlines what information users need throughout the workflow, the delivery mechanisms for that information, and basic guidelines for writing the information.

A good information design strategy results in an information experience that guides users, providing enough information at each stage for them to move through each task efficiently and confidently. Before designing the information strategy, you need to understand the product life cycle and the types of tasks and workflows at each stage in the cycle.

While the product life cycle in marketing terms generally begins with the inception of a product idea and continues until all development ceases, for end users, it begins when they open the package or otherwise start interacting with the application and ends when the application ceases to be used. Following is an example of a product life cycle for an IT administrator product.

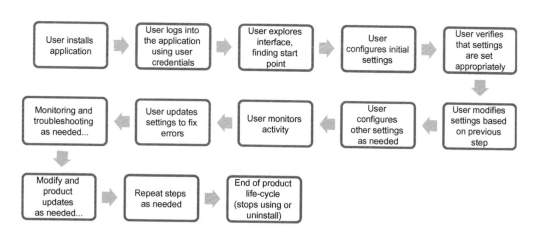

Similarly, the product life cycle for a web application for creating photo albums may look something like this:

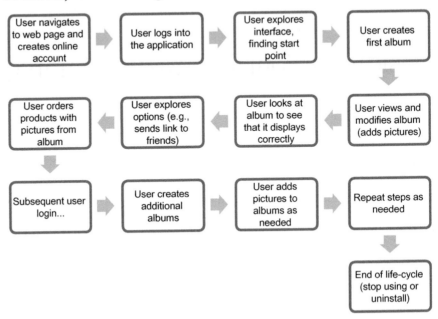

In both of these samples, while the configuration and user tasks are different, both types of applications include similar product life-cycle phases.

UNDERSTANDING THE WORKFLOW PHASES

Throughout the product life cycle and the workflow phases, users may have periods when they interact in a proactive manner, while at other times, user interaction may be reactive. The same is true for how users look for and use information. Understanding when and where you have opportunities to provide this information, and the type of information provided, makes up your information strategy.

Getting Started Phase

The getting started phase is referred to as the first-time user experience. In this phase, the user begins interacting with the application. If the software is on a CD, the user installs the application and then logs into the application. In the case of a web application, users navigate to the login page where they may be required to create a user account and purchase a subscription to the application, or simply log in using a user name and password they define.

When the application first launches, the user explores the interface, getting acquainted with the overall layout, trying to understand the navigation system, and creating a mental model of how the system is designed.

In this phase the user begins by configuring basic settings that are core to using the application. This may include running a getting started wizard to enter network settings (e.g., network business software), entering personal information required to use the application (e.g., personal productivity application), or simply using the application for the first time (e.g., entertainment applications).

Verification and Modification

After getting through the initial configuration phase, users generally take time to review what they have done to make sure the outcome is as expected. For example, an IT administrator setting up network rules will verify that the rules run as expected and that the implementation integrates smoothly into the overall network. A home user creating a photo album of his last vacation may browse through the album to see that the pictures display correctly and are in the right order. This is the time when users are making adjustments and are reviewing what they have done, until they are satisfied with the outcome.

Savvy computer users may also start looking around the application, seeing what other features are available, and begin configuring other core settings.

Ongoing Configuration and Interaction Phase

After the users verify the outcome of their first actions, they begin to build up confidence with the application, assuming that they are on the right path. Next, they become interested in what else the product has to offer. They start exploring and configuring settings that require additional knowledge. The tasks at this stage may be secondary tasks. For example, in the case of an online photo album example, the users may create additional albums and may also begin using the available photo editing tools and adding captions and callouts to their photos.

Network administrators may begin exploring and configuring the advanced options and settings. At this point, the user understands the connection between the different elements and begins navigating the system with more confidence, using system shortcuts.

As users become more familiar and comfortable with the product, there will be ample instances when they will find themselves confused and in need of guidance—and there are ample opportunities within the user interface to provide that guidance.

Maintenance Phase

At various times in the life cycle of a product, there may be instances when users don't actively interact with the application—although they may spend time monitoring or reviewing their settings. And at some point even the savviest users will probably experience some kind of glitch with the system: Changes made to the network may result in something not working, or they may inadvertently delete a required file or setting. This is the time when users try to figure out what went wrong, and they come up with ways to fix or mitigate the problem. During this period, users may need to react to notifications, warning and error messages, alerts, and events. The information you provide in the messages should help users understand not only what is wrong, but also how to solve the problem or issue.

Getting Users Over the Learning Curve

Often the information you provide helps users not only to understand how to interact with the application, but also how to get through the phases, reducing the learning curve as the users move from one task and phase to the next.

The learning curve effect specifies that each time a task is performed, the amount of time required for the next iteration is reduced.

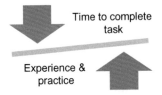

The concept that learning curves, or learning rates, can be represented as a mathematical measurement was introduced by T. P. Wright in 1936 when he published an article describing how the repetition of tasks affects cost estimates. In his article Wright stated that with practice workers become more efficient, and therefore the amount of time required to manufacture an item decreases with time. In his hypothesis, Wright suggested that the amount of time, or man-hours, decreases by a constant percentage each time the production quantity is doubled. Since then, learning curves have been applied to many industries, and numerous equations have been created to measure learning percentages and their effect on time and cost.

In the practical world of application design, we're concerned less with the mathematical value of the learning curve than with how the relationship between experience and the efficiency of completing user tasks affects the learnability and usability of the application. While improving the learning curve may ultimately have a cost benefit to the user, the impact of getting users over the learning curve quickly is paramount to a successful user experience and the overall success of the product. This is particularly true for web applications: If the application is difficult to understand and another similar application is available, users will simply move on to a product that is easier to use. In a business application, where a product has been purchased, users have a higher incentive to work harder to learn the system. Just as you only have one chance to create a first impression when meeting someone, the first impression of your application should be as favorable as possible. On one hand, if the initial interaction with the product is frustrating and difficult to learn, user satisfaction will be negatively affected. On the other hand, if the initial interaction is successful and guides the user through the learning curve, user satisfaction will be high and users will be more apt to recommend and continue using your products.

The best way for users to experience a short learning curve is to provide an application that is intuitive and self-explanatory, and that guides users through the experience until they are ready to do it on their own.

The challenge is to identify the areas where users need help and the right delivery mechanism for the information.

CREATING AN INFORMATION EXPERIENCE STRATEGY

At each stage in the product life cycle, the information required and the delivery mechanism depend on the user's skill level and immediate needs. When creating your strategy, follow these steps to guide you in making the right choices for your users.

1. Identify the target tasks and target areas.
2. Select the delivery mechanisms.
3. Design the implementation model.

Identifying the Target Tasks and Target Areas

In a perfect UX world, every application would be intuitive and easy to use from the first time the user opened the first screen. You can help create that world by making sure the controls in the user interface text—for example, buttons, menu options, and labels—are comprehensible and consistent. Even the best designed applications have some points in the workflow when users are going to need information that the controls cannot provide. Identifying these areas, and then finding the right way to supply the information, will help users through these steps.

Although each application is different, here are some typical times in the workflow, or areas, when users may need additional information to complete their tasks:

Target Tasks and Areas	User Issues
Installing and logging in	Following the installation sequence
	Creating a user account and logging into the application
Configuring initial configuration settings	Understanding how to get started with the application (first task)
Completing core tasks	Understanding the workflow and settings for tasks that are core, or required, for using the application
Completing tasks across features	Understanding the process when a single task requires users to configure settings in different locations within the interface.
Navigating and discovering	Understanding the visual presentation of the navigation hierarchy
	Understanding iconography and suggested workflow as visually presented
	Finding the options for a specific task
Configuring advanced settings and workflows	Configuring settings that require additional knowledge outside the basic, core competencies
Monitoring	Understanding how monitoring information is provided and displayed
	Reacting to monitoring information
Troubleshooting	Understanding how to respond to notifications and alerts in the system
	Exploring troubleshooting tools
	Finding information online

By understanding where users may require additional guidance, you can begin thinking about what information they need and the methods used to provide that information. Depending on the complexity of an application, there may be many more target areas. In addition, usability testing and user feedback will provide crucial information about the specific stages and steps that are problematic for your users.

Looking at the table, your next step is to consider the information required to help users through the areas and tasks you identified. The tricky part here is thinking about the scope of information you should include and using the right delivery mechanism. Overloading a page with information, however relevant you think it is, may actually confuse the user. The general rule is to provide only enough information for the user to complete the task.

In this example, it's difficult to discern how the information helps the users decide whether they want to turn on the feature and what it actually does.

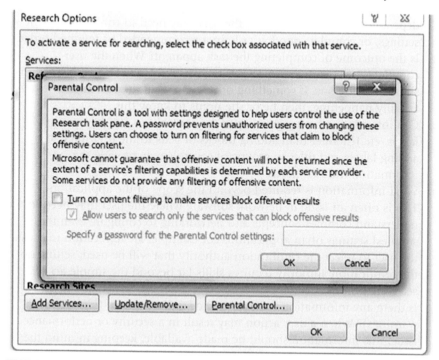

FIGURE 9.1 Too much text is difficult to read.

Information and instruction within the user interface are meant to help users through tasks, not to document the features. And keep in mind that users generally read only enough information to go on to the next step. Providing information they may need several steps later is not helpful and may overwhelm them.

Avoid the temptation to document the application within the user interface.

To determine what information the user needs at a specific step, it's helpful to ask yourself these questions:

1. What does the user need to know to complete this task? This question is related to the application design, not to the user's skill level (see number 5 below). For example, if the program requires the user to enter the

administrator password to save the settings, he or she should be aware of this requirement prior to starting the task at hand.

2. Does the task need to be completed in a specific order? When there are dependencies between settings, the user may need to configure specific settings, or complete another task, in a recommended or required order.

3. Is the outcome of completing the task apparent? When the user completes a task or confirms a setting, the outcome of his or her actions should be obvious. If something other than what the user expects is actually happening, then he or she needs to know this.

4. Can information be integrated into the control text (titles, grouping, labels, etc.)? Rather than adding blocks of texts to the user interface, adding labels and titles to groups of controls may provide the information the user needs.

5. What information is required beyond the scope of the application? This is often an issue in network software where the user may need to understand complex concepts and networking to configure even the simplest settings of an application. For example, an application may ask the user to select the certification authority that will be used; setting up the certification authority requires skills far beyond the simple act of selecting it from a list.

6. Is there any information the user's needs to be aware of (e.g., security warnings)? When a user action may result in a security or performance issue, this information should be made available, keeping in mind the user's knowledge levels.

7. Is the task core to the application? When deciding how to prioritize resources and the time investment, you may need to focus on the core tasks.

Selecting the Information Delivery Mechanism

After you have created your list of target tasks and areas for which information is required, and defined the information needs for that task, you decide on the delivery methods for the information and how it will be integrated into the user interface. While you are working with the UX designer on the overall look and feel of the content integration, you should also work with the technical writers on the specific text strings and decide which content is better suited for a help topic or document.

Generally speaking, all user interface text is a form of embedded instruction—helping users understand the controls and settings provided in a page, and helping them use the options to complete tasks. New and creative ways of integrating content into the user interface, in particular in web applications and for mobile devices, are becoming increasingly popular when the user interface text cannot provide all the information users need to interact success-fully with the application.

While the formatting may differ based on the hardware and software being used, there are delivery mechanisms, for example, content types, which are most often used for adding another layer of instruction to an application.

Landing Pages

Landing pages are an ideal location for adding instructions and guidance into the user interface, introducing terminology, and providing quick links to common or required tasks. When designed properly, landing pages can help describe the application workflow and navigation model.

In the following sample, you can see how adding content and links to the page (on the right) provides guidance as well as an opportunity to help users understand the options available in the navigation tree on the left.

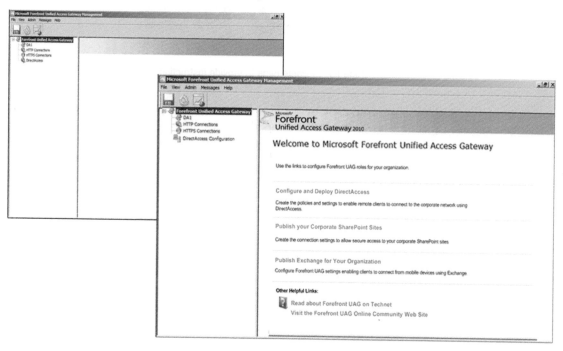

In a web application, the landing page, often referred to as the *welcome page*, is the first page the user sees when logging in. In the next example, you can see how this page provides navigational guidance by providing a button in the middle of the page. You can also see that the page provides step-by-step instruction, with quick links to those steps. Both of these approaches are helpful to the first-time user.

FIGURE 9.2 Using the welcome page to provide instruction.

Note, however, that by providing two starting points (for example, in the picture above, the button and the quick steps), users may be confused as to which one they should choose. Giving users too many ways to complete the same action can have the opposite effect of what you are trying to accomplish.

Wizards

Wizards are useful for walking users through a sequence of steps, providing instruction and help as part of the flow of the wizard. Since users must go through the pages in the order provided, wizards are particularly helpful for guiding users when there are dependencies between settings. In the following example, the selections made in one page impact the options presented in subsequent pages.

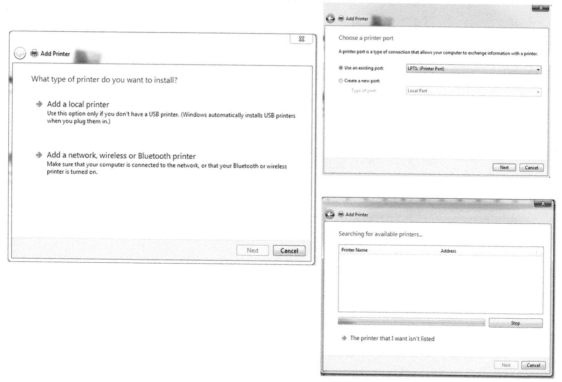

FIGURE 9.3 Wizards walk the user through a sequence.

Getting Started wizards are a successful tool for walking users through the initial configuration of an application, ensuring that each step is completed and validated along the way.

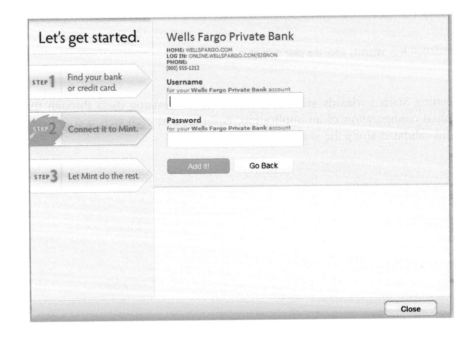

Because wizards are considered a form of help, access to the product help is not always available from a wizard page. You can provide additional information by including help links in the page. Keep in mind that help links embedded in a wizard should lead the user to information that is relevant and necessary for helping users select the appropriate options and input text for the task at hand.

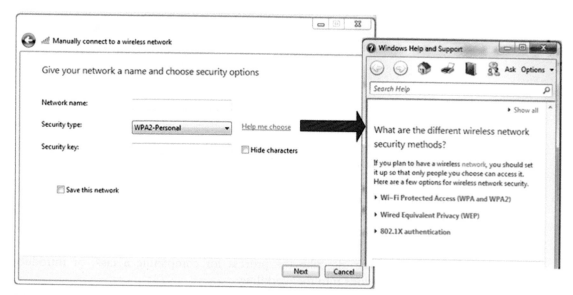

FIGURE 9.4 Example of a help link in a wizard page.

Occasionally, users will need information that is not part of a particular step in a wizard but is crucial for them to know before continuing. When this happens, you can add an informational page to the wizard. This isn't something you should do often, but it is effective if you want to be sure users are aware of specific issues, such as completing an action outside of the wizard before continuing on to the next step in the wizard.

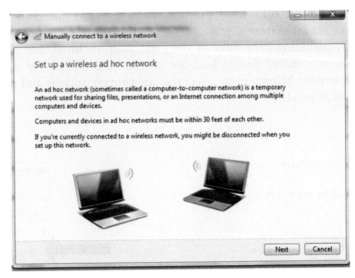

FIGURE 9.5 Example of an informational wizard page.

Embedded Instruction

Beyond the standard text and labels used within a typical interface, you may find places where additional instruction can be embedded directly into the user interface. This embedded instruction may help users through the first-time experience, describe the process for completing a task, or introduce recommendations into the workflow.

Embedded instruction can be provided in many formats, depending on the device and type of application, and can be provided directly in the user interface, or as callouts and help balloons. In this example, simple callouts are used to instruct the user through a single task.

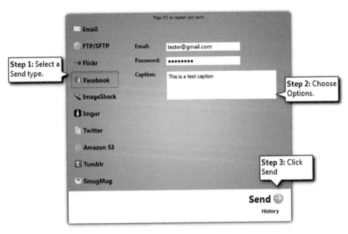

FIGURE 9.6 Callouts showing a process.

Callouts can also be used to direct users to a single starting point and then lead them through each step in a task, presenting the next callout when the previous step is completed.

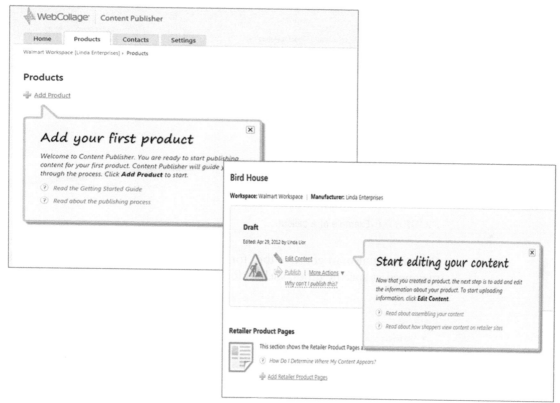

FIGURE 9.7 Callouts presented sequentially.

Web applications often use callouts that inform users of features they may not be aware of, helping them take advantage of options that may not be part of the core workflow.

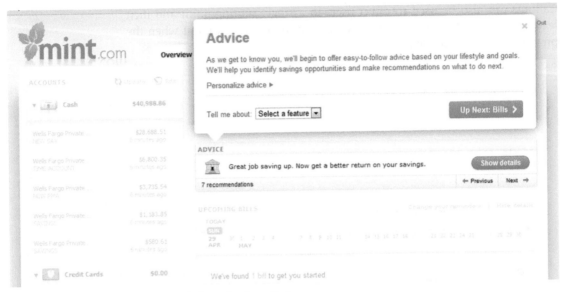

FIGURE 9.8 Example of a callout.

Callouts are also an effective tool for drawing attention to information users may need at specific times, such as for system notifications and alerts.

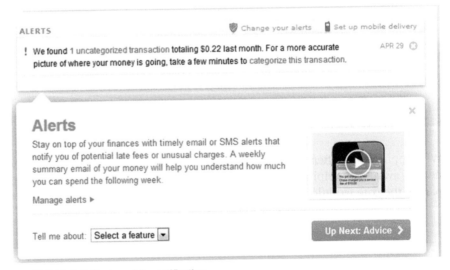

FIGURE 9.9 Callout used for notification.

Demos and Tutorials

Providing a short demo or preview of how to use the application is a friendly way to let users know what to expect and how to get started using the application. Demos can require users to click through the steps, or they can run automatically. Because demos are not interactive, the level of detail should be kept minimal: The purpose is to provide an overview of the process or concepts.

Demos and tutorials are particularly good ways to provide information when step-by-step instructions and the application can be viewed together, helping users complete a process at the same time.

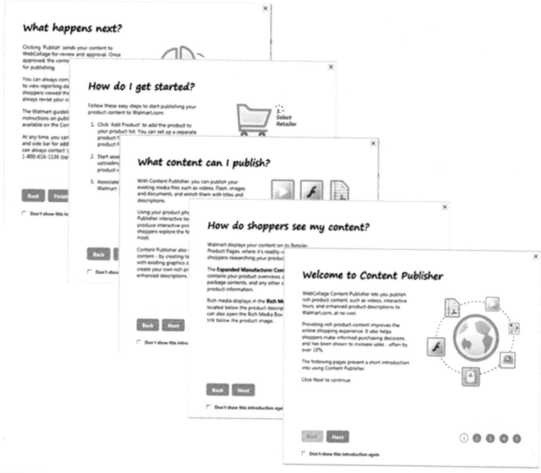

FIGURE 9.10 Example of demo pages.

Context-Sensitive Help

Embedding help into the application is a good way to provide information for users who want and need it, without adding large blocks of text directly into the user interface. Context-sensitive help links may open any of the following: a help box with a short explanation, a help topic in the product help, or a help page on the Internet.

Users should have some indication as to what kind of help a link or button will open, either by the link's formatting or by the text used to access the content. One benefit of linking to a help topic on the Internet is that content can be updated and modified on an ongoing basis rather than as part of a software update. The downside is that the user must have Internet connectivity to read the help.

Help Buttons and Hyperlinks

There is little difference in functionality between a help button and a help hyperlink. Usually, help buttons are used in warnings and popup messages to provide additional information about the cause of the warning or event.

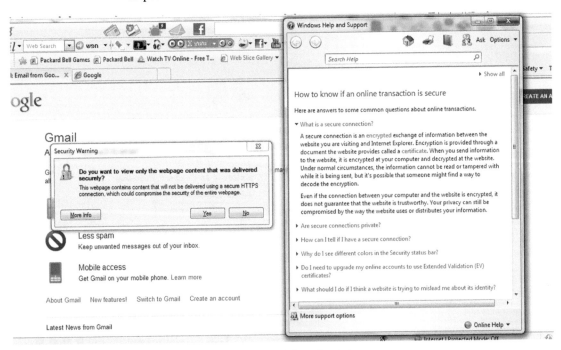

FIGURE 9.11 Example of more information help.

Hyperlinks are useful on landing pages and in wizards and dialogs to provide information about the controls and options in the page.

When implemented properly, help links are a good solution for providing information some users may want to understand before configuring settings, without adding blocks of text to the interface. In the next example, the information is available but not required. When adding help links to the user interface, it should be clear what kind of information will be displayed and to which controls the link is related.

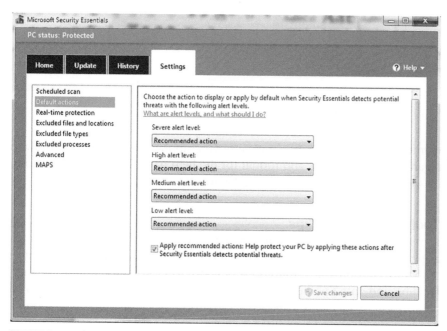

FIGURE 9.12 Example of a help link.

Help Panes

Many applications are designed with an action pane or a help pane, placed in a sidebar on each main page of the application. This is a good location for providing quick links to the relevant topics in the product help or to supplementary documents and videos.

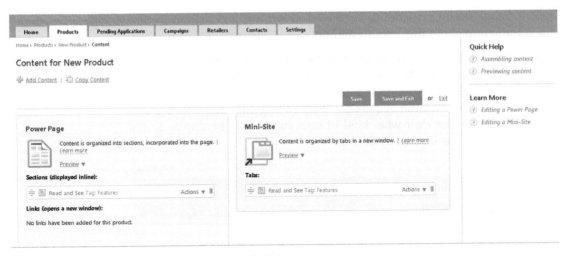

FIGURE 9.13 Example of a help pane.

If you decide to include a help pane in your application, think about how to organize the help topics and format for the help pane. Then you can customize the topics for each page in the interface.

Tooltips and Info-Tips

Tooltips provide descriptive text, such as labels, and short explanations for graphical objects, such as icons in toolbars and ribbons. Info-tips are a type of tooltip, providing descriptions for desktop, window, and menu commands. Tooltips and info-tips are simple and effective ways to provide additional information for elements dispersed throughout a product.

In web applications, tooltips and info-tips are being used to call attention to new, or changed, features and options. This is an effective way to let users know about improved or additional features, or tasks that may otherwise go unnoticed.

FIGURE 9.14 Example of an info-tip.

Integration with Other Sources of Information

A good information experience will undoubtedly include documents and other collateral materials, depending on the technical specifications and complexity of the application. Quick start guides, installation manuals, knowledge base (kb) articles, and white papers may all be part of the total information pack. In addition, the company web site will undoubtedly contain explanations and descriptions of how the application works and what it does.

Since the information experiences all fit together to create a single combined user experience, it's important to pay attention to the information provided in print, in the online help, and wherever else information appears. Specifically, make sure the following are consistent across information channels:

- *Terminology:* A single terminology list should be created for all teams as a reference.
- *User workflows:* Defining user scenarios for the main workflows, and then using these as a reference across materials will help everyone stay aligned.
- *Recommended settings and options:* Default settings provided in the user interface should be considered the recommended settings for most users. Use these settings in diagrams, screen captures, and user guides.
- *Marketing messages:* If the marketing team is promoting the product in a specific direction, then all other materials should adhere to the same messaging.

Social Media

In recent years, social media, such as Facebook, LinkedIn, Twitter, wikis, and team blogs, have become popular vehicles for distributing information to users. The informal nature of social media makes it easy for anyone to add and update information as needed.

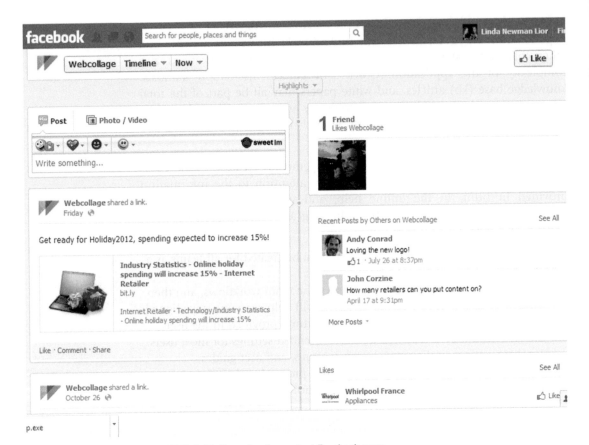

FIGURE 9.15 Example of a product Facebook page.

Information that is spread through social media becomes part of the total information experience. As such, it's important to make sure it adheres to the same standards applied to the application, user interface text, print materials, and any other information distributed by the company. Terminology, marketing themes, and the quality of the writing should all be consistent. And while the writing may be informal, it should be grammatically and technically correct.

DESIGNING THE IMPLEMENTATION MODEL

Now that you are familiar with the different information delivery mechanisms, here are guidelines for how each content type is best used. Use this table to help decide which delivery mechanisms are best suited for each task in the workflow:

Delivery Mechanism Use Table	
Use. . ..	**To. . .**
Landing Pages	Improve discoverability
	Provide navigation shortcuts to required tasks
	Introduce new terms
	Show a process
Wizards	Complete a task in a required order
	Walk users through complex tasks
Callouts	Improve discoverability
	Show a workflow
Help Panes	Provide links to information outside the user interface
	Provide links to videos and other information on the Internet
Context-sensitive help	Provide additional information that will help users complete the task they are working on
Demos and tutorials	Provide an overview of the process
	Introduce concepts users will need to understand
Tooltips and info-tips	Provide descriptions for graphical elements such as icons
	Call attention to new features and options

Creating the implementation strategy depends on time and resources. You may find that you have to limit your delivery mechanisms and the amount of content you integrate into the application. Each delivery mechanism requires planning, developer resources, testing, and follow-up. One way to decide where to put your efforts is to create "rings of quality" and then prioritize the information needs according to each ring.

DEFINING RINGS OF QUALITY

The idea behind rings of quality is that not all parts of the user interface, or workflow, are created equally. Tasks that are core to the product (that most users will interact with or configure) have a higher rating than, for example, advanced tasks that only a small percentage of users will configure.

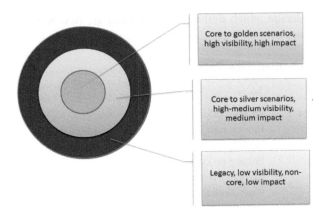

Core to golden scenarios, high visibility, high impact

Core to silver scenarios, high-medium visibility, medium impact

Legacy, low visibility, non-core, low impact

FIGURE 9.16 The rings of quality concept.

There are different ways to define your rings of quality, but one simple way is to determine the impact of that element on the overall user experience as an Experience Profile (EP) quotient.

Experience Profile (EP)	Used Frequently	Used Infrequently
Many Users	EP1	EP2
Few Users	EP2	EP3

The EP quotient for a feature, or task, is defined by the number of users who will interact with the feature and the frequency of that interaction. Through this method, tasks or user interface elements with the highest EP (i.e., EP1) are considered Gold tasks, EP2 are Silver, and EP3 are low impact, or Bronze.

Determining the EP quotient for your tasks and workflows will help you prioritize and decide which tasks to focus on when implementing your information strategy, and how you will deliver the information. You should focus on tasks with the high EP.

There is one more factor that is not included in the EP table: features (or tasks) that all users must complete or interact with one time only. For example, installing or downloading the application, or configuring a setting that is core to running the application (e.g., Gateway IP address, ISP for networking applications). Your content strategy should include a mechanism for getting users through these tasks as smoothly as possible and with a stellar success rate.

Localization
Localization refers to translating an application into languages other than the language in which it was developed. You can localize a product into one or

many languages. Keep in mind that language affects the length of text, and you will need to allow 30 percent extra space for translation. For example, in German, the word "edit" becomes *Bearbeiten*. "Sort ascending" becomes *Lajittele nousevassa järjestyksessä* in Finnish.

This means that your user interface text will take up much more space than you anticipated, depending on the language. It also means that you will need to build the interactive text so that the strings can be easily sent out for translation.

Note: Keep in mind that consistent terminology makes translation easier and less costly. Localization guidelines are included in the next section.

User Skill Levels and Task Difficulty

In the previous chapter, we discussed understanding your users and personas. When deciding how to expend your resources creating the information experience, keep in mind the skill and knowledge levels of your users and how these levels impact their information needs. Providing highly technical information is not required for a consumer product, unless the user is able to do something with that information. Providing simplistic explanations for complex features used only by advanced users won't have value added, and your time and resources can be better spent elsewhere.

PUTTING IT ALL TOGETHER

Now that you've identified the user workflows and tasks, and have determined the EP levels of each task, you can decide how to integrate the information into the user experience.

For example, you may create a table that looks something like this for each task or workflow:

| Task | First-time Experience—Creating First Item | | | |
	Issues	Difficulty Level	EP	Delivery Mechanism
Creating photo album	Navigation and discoverability	Easy	1	Callout
Adding photo to album	Discoverability	Easy	1	Callout
Saving album	Discoverability	Easy	1	Callout
...				

Or if you know that the task will be performed using a wizard, you may create a table outlining the information needs for each page in that wizard:

Initial Network Settings (Wizard)—Steps Must Be Completed in This Order				
Task	**Issues**	**Difficulty Level**	**EP**	**Delivery Mechanism**
Welcome page	*Discoverability*	–	1	Link to wizard from landing
Adding network IP addresses	*Navigation and discoverability*	Complex	1	Help link
Adding a workgroup or domain	*Discoverability*	Complex	1	Help link
Selecting a network template	*Terminology and concept*	Mid	1	Help link
Saving settings	–	Easy	1	–

As you create your tables or charts, you will need to work with the product team to determine milestones and schedules. You will also need to work with the product designer and technical writers (if you are lucky enough to have them), on the design and text strings.

Your next step is to create the specifications for each information type. This is covered in the next chapter.

WHAT ARE THE KEY COMPONENTS OF A POSITIVE INFORMATION EXPERIENCE?

Sharon (Hauser) Ainspan
Chief Usability Officer at TentLearn ContTented Learners (Israel and USA)

The key components of a positive information experience are, essentially, directly correlated with the impressions your audience would (ideally) have, during and after the experience:

"Most of what I needed was right there in the first place." (Information needs and priorities are anticipated.)

"I did not have to waste time figuring out how to get additional information." (Panels/links are optimally laid out.)

"I have found what I was looking for (and maybe even a bit more, but did not have to filter through extraneous information)." (Information overload is avoided.)

"It is presented clearly so I am not confused and I will probably not need to relearn it at a future time." (Proper information architecture, grid, and language are on the page/surface.)

"That diagram really helps me see how all the pieces fit together." (Adequate use is made of schematics and labeling.)

"I see how this topic relates to the other topics/items/tasks I need to know about." (Entity-relationship diagrams and texts are provided.)

"I know where I will be able to look for further detail, or for the larger picture, if and when I need it." (Information hierarchy is clear.)

SUMMARY

The information experience strategy describes the information users need throughout the workflow and discusses the delivery mechanisms for that information. By planning an information strategy, you can provide an experience that gets users over the initial learning curve and through all the phases of the user workflow.

- Planning your information strategy includes defining the content types for your application.
- The phases of the user experience workflow can be described as: getting started (initial configuration), verification and modification, ongoing configuration and interaction, and maintenance.
- When creating your information strategy, follow these basic steps: Identify target tasks, select delivery mechanisms, and design the implementation model.
- Remember that your content is meant to guide the user through tasks, not document the application.
- Always keep in mind the skill and knowledge levels of your users and how these impact their information needs.

CHAPTER 10

Writing Text for Interaction

INTRODUCTION

Your application's user interface tells your product story: The pages and surfaces your users view and interact with throughout the experience explain how the story fits together. Each surface consists of a collection of textual elements: explanations, instructions, titles, labels, interactive buttons and options, hyperlinks, and metaphors used in graphics. The text you provide for these elements is the glue that holds the story together, guiding your users through the various stages of their interaction with the application. Landing pages introduce the main concepts of the story, wizards guide users through the main processes, and property sheets and dialogs present the options required to set up and use the application.

In previous chapters we looked at the "C's" of good user interface text for creating content that is easy to read and understand. In this chapter we'll look at the "A's" of writing which are crucial for providing content users' needs, at the time they need it. By creating text that is both readable and written for interaction, you will provide your users a comprehensive, positive information experience.

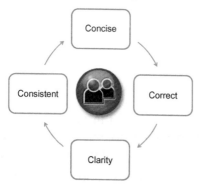

FIGURE 10.1 The C's of writing.

FIGURE 10.2 The A's of writing.

THE FOUR A'S OF WRITING

While the four C's of good writing revolve around writing content that is easily scanned and read, the A's of writing focus on building text that guides and assists your users.

When users reach a page in your application, they should intuitively understand what tasks are available and the actions for completing the task. When deciding where to place your text and when writing the content, applying the "A's" of writing means asking yourself these questions:

Available	Where and when does the user need the information?
Actionable	Does the information help users understand what to do?
Assistive	Does the information help users understand the task or workflow?
Appropriate	Does the text provide the right amount and level of information?

Available Content

When writing your text, it's important to provide the information the user needs, when and where they need it. Your information is there to help users make decisions, move forward in their workflow, and understand the application. If the information exists, but is not available at the right time or in a location, you have missed your opportunity for supporting your users.

The examples below show examples of how you can make content available, helping users through a workflow, understanding the options, and providing recommendations.

In the past few years, many tools have become available for building a layer of guidance, such as help callouts into your application.

In this example, the callouts automatically appear at each step in the flow.

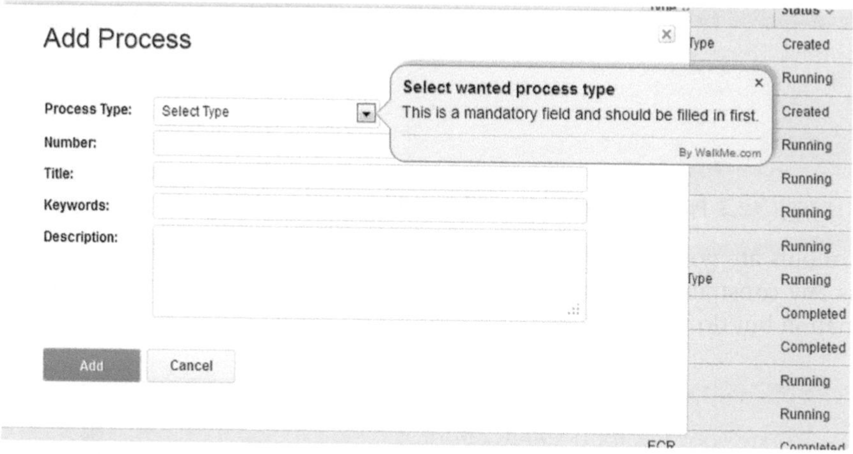

FIGURE 10.3 Using callouts helps users through a process.

The callouts help the user understand the requirements and make sure they complete the steps in the required order.

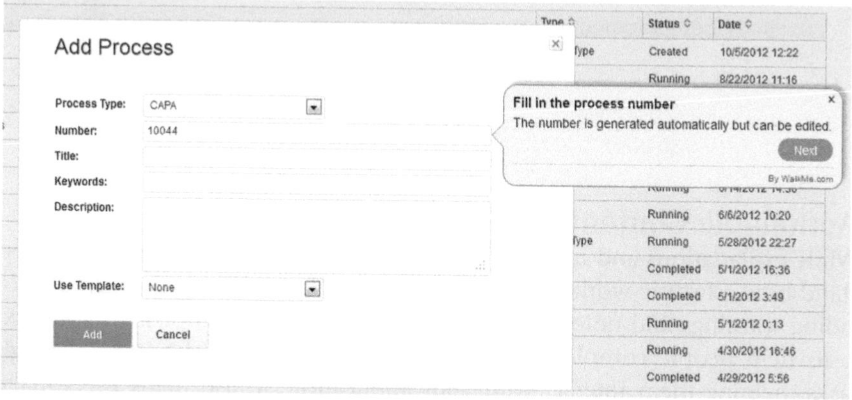

FIGURE 10.4 Using callouts to complete the process.

Built-in assistance can also let users know the constraints and recommendations for specific fields and options.

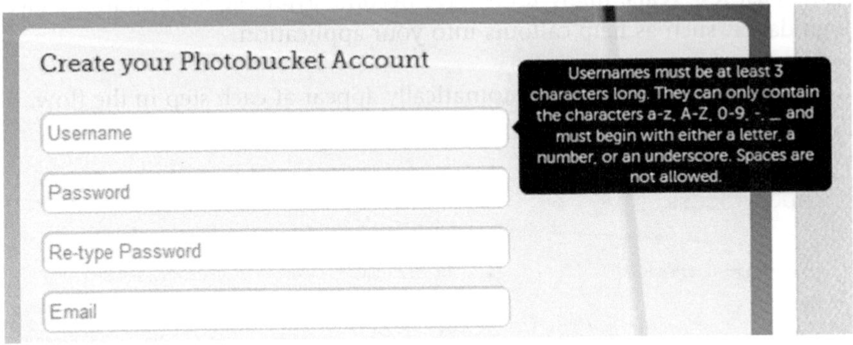

FIGURE 10.5 Providing field input directions in callouts.

Callouts are good for letting users know what to expect at each step, as well as any constraints and recommendations. The callouts provide useful information but do not interfere.

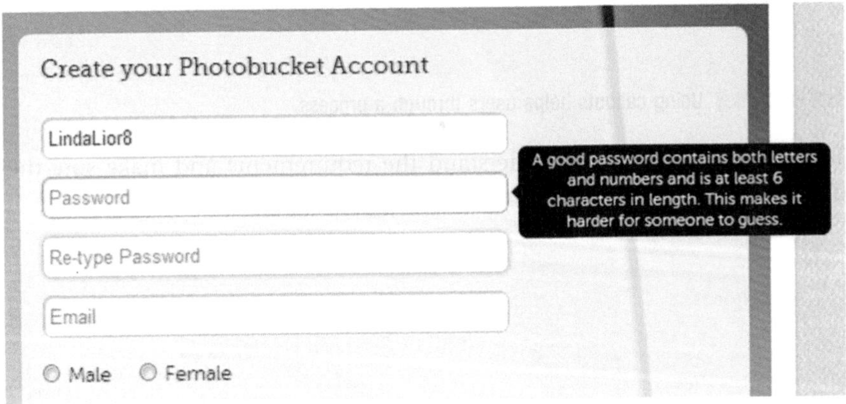

Actionable Content

While explanations and informational text are useful for helping users understand how a feature works and what options are available, as well as for providing warnings and notes, keep in mind that the main purpose of your text is to help people complete tasks. Actionable content guides users through tasks, helping them interact with your application; it also helps users make choices and move through workflows.

In the following page, the writer combines explanatory and actionable instruction. Notice that the text in the heading and in the paragraph that follows describes the interaction from the users' perspective. The button label clearly indicates what will happen when the user clicks the button.

Help people tag you in photos and videos

By turning on Find My Face, Google+ can prompt people you know to tag your face when it appears in photos and videos.

Of course, you have control over which tags you accept or reject, and you can turn this feature on or off in Google+ settings. Learn more

Turn on Find My Face   No Thanks

FIGURE 10.6 Writing actionable text.

Actionable content should provide enough text for users to understand the action they should take and the result of that interaction. In the following example, users don't need to know anything beyond the information provided.

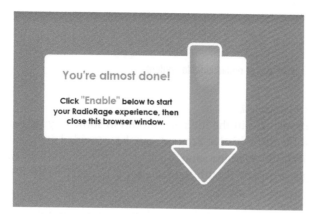

FIGURE 10.7 Example of actionable text prompts.

What Is Nonactionable Content?

Although some explanatory information is helpful, keeping in mind that your main goal is to promote user interaction with the application will help you avoid pages like the following one. In this page, the writer tries to explain the feature, but none of the text guides the user toward action. The page would be much more helpful if it included instructions or examples rather than explanations.

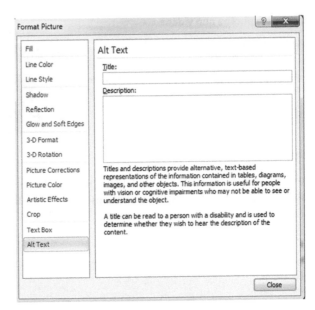

FIGURE 10.8 Example of nonactionable content.

Assistive Content

Each string of text within the interface should in some way help users interact with your software. Assistive content can be provided in a variety of formats—notifications, callouts, and hover text are all familiar ways to help your users get acquainted with your features, move through a task, or proceed from one task to another.

While short explanations such as subtitles and prompts often provide enough guidance within a page, you may find that some workflows are more complex than others, and users could benefit from additional, assistive guidance. Assistance guidance integrated into a workflow is becoming increasingly common within web applications in particular.

Although the callouts in the previous examples helped users enter information into fields, in the following example, the callout text helps the users understand the workflow, letting them know that the previous task was completed and telling them how to proceed to the next logical step in the sequence. This is a good example of how you can guide users toward completing a series of tasks.

FIGURE 10.9 Example of guided assistance.

Notice that while the text in this callout suggests the next step, it doesn't force the user to take the action. This is a good example of how you can recommend a workflow to the user, while allowing flexibility.

When tasks require users to complete the steps in a specific sequence, without flexibility, you can integrate a step-by-step callout sequence within your interface, allowing users to move only in the required order of steps. When steps must be completed in a specific order, wizards are also an optional form of assistance.

Appropriate Content

In previous chapters we spoke about using the right tone, which is one component of appropriate writing. Another component is making sure your content provides the right concepts and level of information for your users.

Every label, string, and piece of information in your pages should be relevant for the target user. Avoid the tendency to overexplain concepts within the user interface, and avoid technical jargon. This helps you reduce redundant text and create pages that are easier to read and scan.

Appropriate content provides the right amount of information, where and how it is effective for your users.

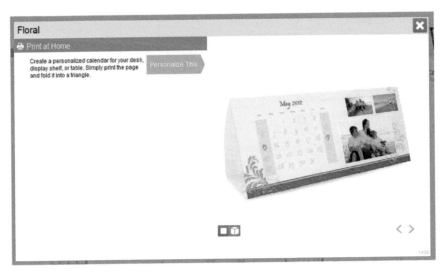

FIGURE 10.10 Example of appropriate level of content.

If the information is important, providing a link to a help topic is a preferable method for presenting detailed explanations and technical concepts.

MAPPING INFORMATION TO THE USER WORKFLOW

Matching the flow of the information to the order in which the user needs the information, or the order in which the task is presented, helps users understand the connection between the options, workflow, and the text in the page.

Landing pages are good for presenting high-level information about main features and providing links for drilling down into the options and help for that feature. Explanations and short descriptions within the user interface are an effective way of teaching users about using your application, introducing new terminology, and describing what options and features offer.

Landing pages help users understand a workflow or aid in selecting a specific path when a sequence of steps is either recommended or required.

In the next example, the text describes three main options the user may want to use and lets the user know the benefits of each option. The text doesn't suggest any sequence of action or imply that any one option is preferable over another.

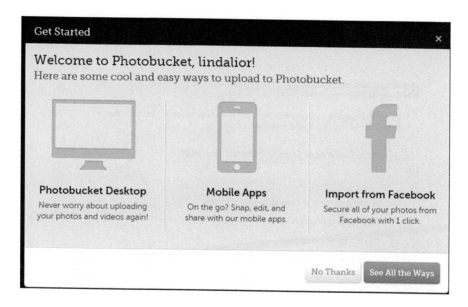

Whether it's a landing page, a property page, or a wizard, planning how your content is placed helps avoid situations where users are presented with a page requiring them to work at figuring out the connection between the information and the settings.

In the following page, the information presented is meant to help the users decide whether or not they want to use HTTPS and to suggest the implications of either selection. However, users will have to work hard to figure out how to interpret the text and how the information fits together with the options.

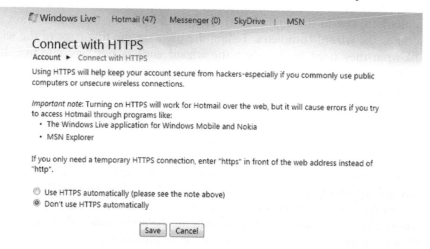

FIGURE 10.11 Sample of content that is difficult to read.

Notice how in this wizard page, the flow of the text, the spacing alignment, and grouping help users understand the connection between the settings.

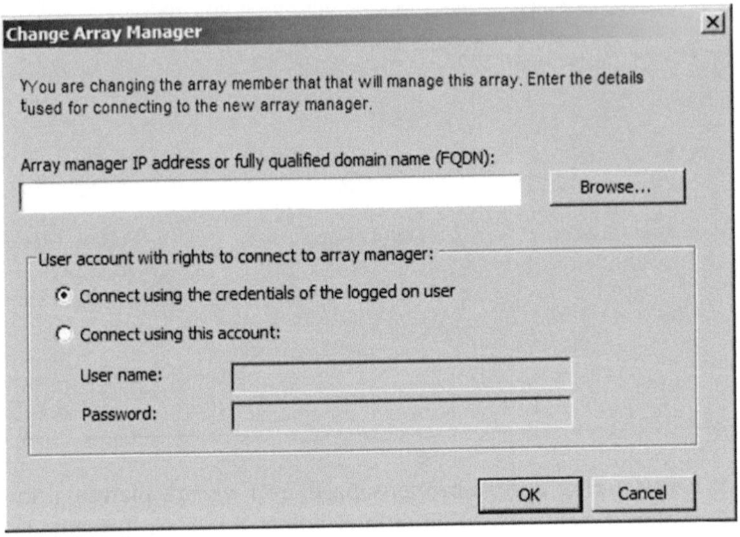

FIGURE 10.12 Sample of well-designed text layout.

Keep in mind that when users complete a wizard, they believe they've completed a process. If, for example, the name of the wizard is the "Setup an Account Wizard," they will assume that when the wizard is completed, the account is set up and ready to use. If any additional steps are required to complete the process (such as restarting the computer or selecting a checkbox somewhere else in the application), you should provide this information as soon as the wizard completes. Telling the users on the first page of the wizard what they need to do when the wizard ends is not very effective: It's highly unlikely they will remember by the time they get to the end of even a short wizard.

FINDING THE RIGHT VOICE

In every conversation, there are different ways to express a single idea. You may say something as a statement, a command, or a suggestion. The same is true for the way you express yourself in the user interface. While it's generally considered good writing practice to write in the active voice, there are times when the passive voice is acceptable, and even preferable.

Active Voice

As the term implies, text written in the active voice is constructed with the subject of the sentence doing the action. The subject is typically the user or a component of the application. Sentences written in the active voice follow this word order: doer of action–action–receiver of action.

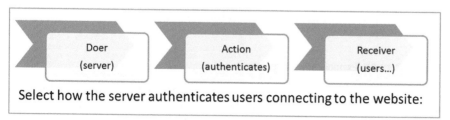

FIGURE 10.13 Example of active voice.

Sentences written in the active voice are less wordy and easier for users to scan, read, and understand. They are also considered more engaging for your users.

There is a common misconception that any sentence using a form of "to be" (e.g., is, are) is not using active voice. This is not always the case, and you may find yourself needing a "to be" verb for letting the user know what will happen when an option is selected.

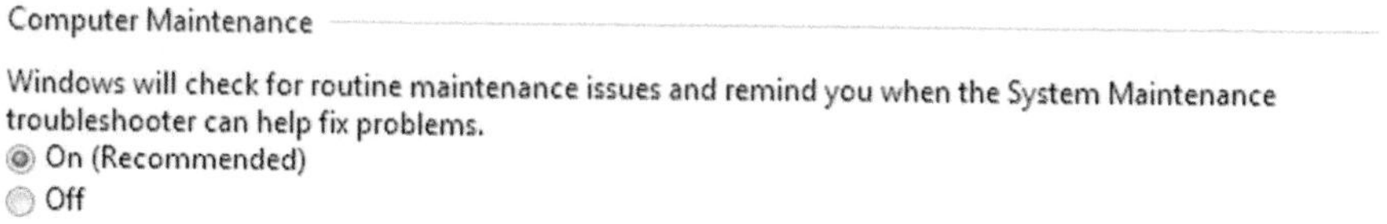

Computer Maintenance

Windows will check for routine maintenance issues and remind you when the System Maintenance troubleshooter can help fix problems.
◉ On (Recommended)
◯ Off

FIGURE 10.14 Using active voice, future tense.

Writing the same message in this way would not result in a sentence that is easier to understand:

Windows checks for routine maintenance issues and reminds you when the System Maintenance troubleshooter helps fix problems.

Passive Voice

Sentences written in the passive voice are constructed in such a way that the subject is being acted upon (the receiver) rather than being the doer of the action. Because passive sentences require additional words and change the usual ordering of a sentence, they tend to make readers work harder to understand the intended meaning.

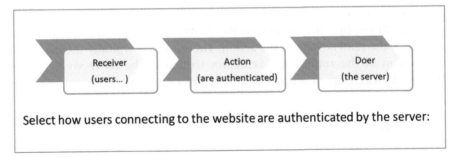

FIGURE 10.15 Example of passive voice.

Although the active voice is a better choice when actions are in the present tense, you may find that passive sentences are better for conveying information without placing blame or responsibility. In the figure on the right, the message implies a problem with the program which may or may not be the case.

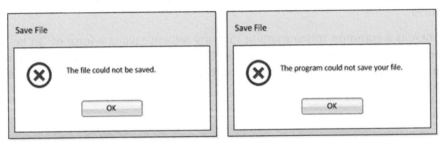

FIGURE 10.16 Example of passive and active message.

In this example, the message on the right, using the active voice, implies that the user may be responsible for the error. In this case, using the passive voice provides a better experience.

Some messages simply read better when written in the passive form. For example, "Your file is being saved" reads better than "The program is saving your file."

Use the passive voice to soften a message when the active voice may place blame or cause the users to feel that you are scolding them. For example, in the samples below, the passive sentence on the left in the following figure is much friendlier than the active voice sentence on the right.

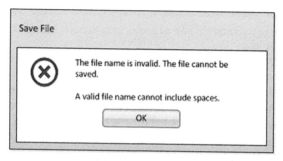

Imperative Voice

Imperative voice gives instructions or commands, or expresses a request. Imperative sentences generally begin with a verb and include ending punctuation. The imperative voice is good when users are required to take action, selecting an option or following a sequence of steps. Examples of imperative voice sentences are as follows:

- Select the users allowed to change the settings.
- Add users to the allowed users list.
- Type a name for the image.
- Follow these steps to complete the action.

Notice in the following wizard page that the subtitle uses the imperative voice to instruct the user. However, when users view the property page, the settings are already configured: They may only be viewing the page. In the corresponding property page, the imperative voice is not used.

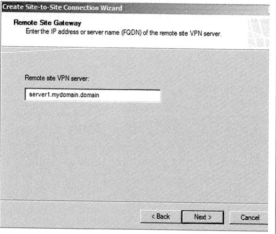

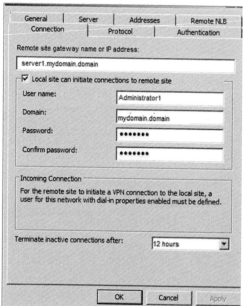

Use the imperative voice when the user is required to take an action, such as select from a list, click a button, or type an entry in a text box.

When writing for web applications, it's important to find the balance between instructing users with the imperative voice and guiding users by using gentler language. One way of finding this balance is to use the nonimperative voice with a friendly and supportive tone for explanations and descriptions, and to use the imperative voice for titles, button labels, and interactive elements.

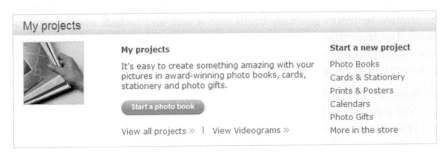

FIGURE 10.17 Using the imperative voice for button labels.

Web applications also have to find the balance between providing relevant information and using the real estate for marketing messages. In particular, if your application is integrated into your company web site, limit your marketing messages and buzz words within the interactive text. Any marketing messages integrated into your text messages should be used sparingly and should be subtle.

FIGURE 10.18 Mixing instruction and marketing (*HP Photo Creations*).

Visual Considerations

When designing and writing your information, think about how your user will read the page and use the options. Remember to take a holistic look at the page. Will the user scan the page as you intended? Are the options in the correct order?

For example, in the following page, the explanatory text and bullet points are clearly written, appropriate, and relevant. However, the arrow toward the bottom of the page is distracting, drawing the user to information that is irrelevant and confusing given that the same action already exists in a button on the page.

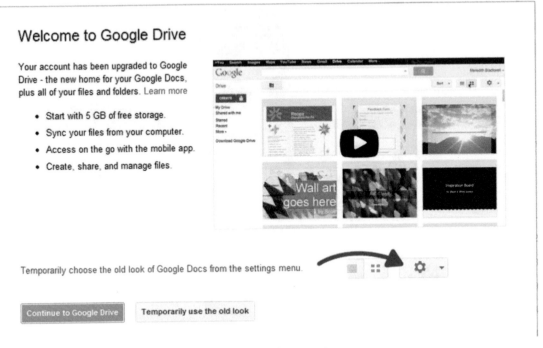

FIGURE 10.19 Sample of distracting content.

The next example shows how, in this case, visuals help users understand the task, with very little text.

FIGURE 10.20 Sample of first-time user experience (*Zazzle.com*).

WRITING THE USER INTERFACE ELEMENTS

Now that you understand the concepts and ideas behind writing user interface text, it's time to start writing the actual text. The next sections provide guidelines and examples that will help you write the content within the user interface.

Writing Title Bars

Title bars help users to continue being oriented to where they are in the application. Remember that your users may be in the midst of several activities and may have multiple windows open on their monitors. The text you use for the title bar will help them keep focused on the task they are completing in that page. As such, the text should correspond directly to the command, link or to whatever element they interacted with to arrive on that page.

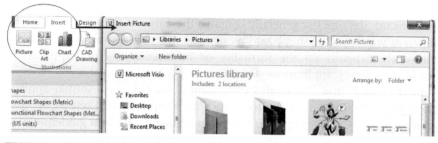

FIGURE 10.21 Example of a title bar.

Title bars should be as specific as possible. As in the next example, when you have generic command button labels, such as Settings, Delete, Add, and Edit, it's easier for your users if you include the name of the feature or action in the title (e.g., Delete Image, Add Label, Edit Colors).

In this example, the name of the feature is added to the title bar, helping users remember from which option the dialog was accessed.

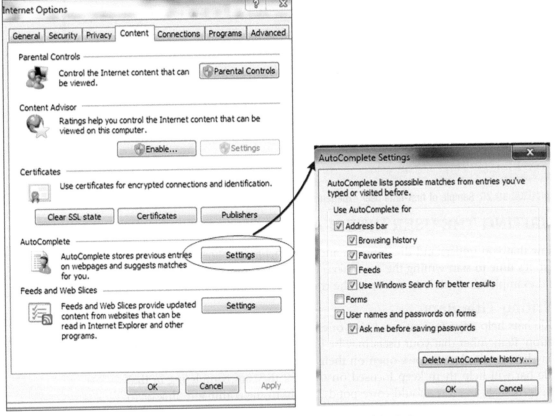

FIGURE 10.22 Title bars should reflect the name of the feature.

In a wizard, the title bar generally contains the name of the wizard. There are different ways to write the wizard name, and whatever format you decide on ultimately depends on the formality or informality of your application. Traditional server applications tend to use a formal tone, that is, "Getting Started Wizard" and "Network Configuration Wizard." Less formal applications generally use a friendlier tone, such as "Getting started setting up your computer" or "Configuring your computer settings." The best guideline is to choose a format and tone that works well for your application and to use it consistently.

Writing Subtitles

Subtitles are useful for describing the overall purpose of a page or section, such as in landing pages and wizards. In the following example, you can see that the subtitle tells the user the purpose of the settings in the page.

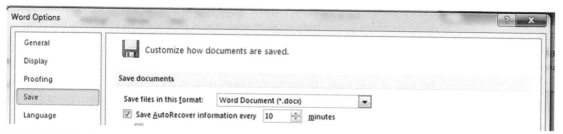

FIGURE 10.23 Example of a subtitle in a software application.

Remember to keep subtitles short and user-focused, helping your users understand the purpose of the page or section.

Explanatory Text

In addition to subtitles, explanatory text describes the features or options presented in the page. Explanations at the top of the page, next to a section, or alongside a control can help users decide if they want to use an option or how to select the option that best suits their needs.

My Videograms

A Videogram turns your pictures and clips into a video with music
that tells a story or celebrates a special occasion.

You do not currently have any in your account.

Create a new Videogram

FIGURE 10.24 Example of explanatory text.

The explanatory text helps users understand the selections available in the page and, optionally, the benefits of using the options.

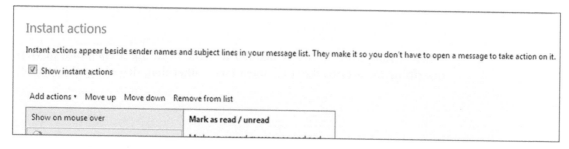

Writing Instructions

Instructional text tells the users what action they should take in the page and provides guidance on how to take that action. The amount of instruction in a page depends on how much information the user needs to complete the action. Some pages many require little or no instructional text, while other, more complex pages may require additional guidance throughout the page.

The location of the instructions depends on the way your pages are built. If the instruction relates to the entire page, then the instruction usually goes at the top of the page. If the instruction relates to a specific control, then the instructions should be placed next to the control, or the instructions can be used as the label for the specific option.

In the following example, the instructional text displays right under the subtitle. The subtitle tells the user the benefits of this feature, while the instructional text tells them what to do.

Find friends from different parts of your life

Use the checkboxes below to discover people you know from your hometown, school, employer and more.

FIGURE 10.25 Example of a subtitle (and explanatory text) in a web application.

In the following example, when there is no subtitle or explanation, the instructions display right next to the relevant field. In this example, the text provides information used to complete the task.

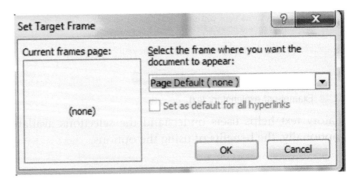

When writing instructions, remember to write from the users' point of view, describing the actions the users must take, rather than describing the feature.

Radio Buttons

Radio buttons are used when the user may select one option from a set of provided alternatives. In many cases, selecting a radio button brings additional options or limits choices. When writing radio button options, you can improve readability by using consistent formatting and avoiding redundancy.

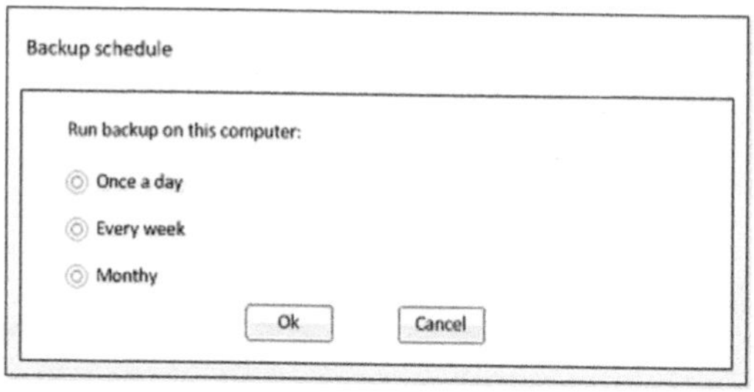

FIGURE 10.26 Inconsistent wording is difficult to read.

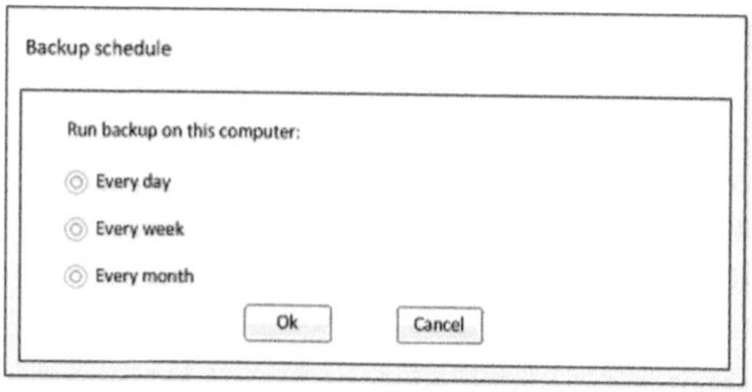

FIGURE 10.27 Wording is consistent but redundant.

In this example, the options are consistently written, and there is no redundant text. Consistent text formatting makes the options easy to scan.

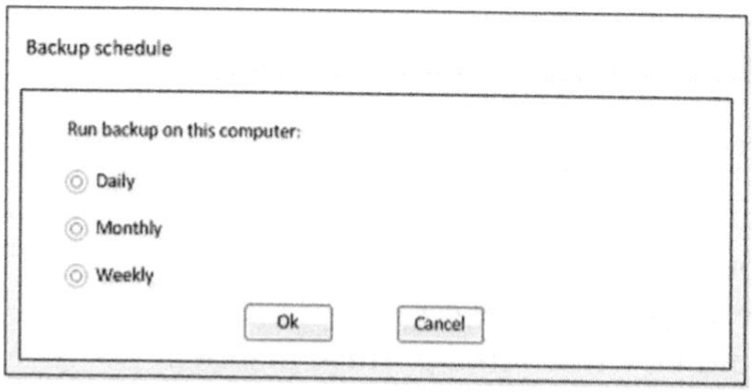

FIGURE 10.28 Consistent and concise labels.

Checkbox Text

Checkboxes are used as a toggle for turning features on or off (enabling or disabling a feature) and are also a common control used for allowing users to select multiple items from a set of options.

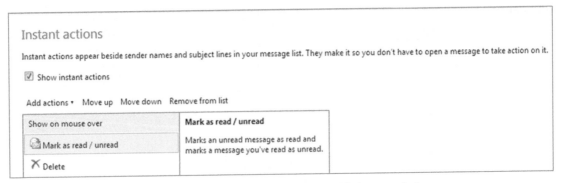

FIGURE 10.29 Example of a checkbox used to turn on a feature.

Checkbox labels should be written in a positive tone, with users selecting the option to enable or turn on a feature rather than disabling a feature. Notice in the next example that each option describes a positive action.

☑	Ignore words in UPPERCASE
☑	Ignore words that contain numbers
☑	Ignore Internet and file addresses
☑	Flag repeated words
☐	Enforce accented uppercase in French
☐	Suggest from main dictionary only

Custom Dictionaries...

French modes: Traditional and new spellings ▼

Spanish modes: Tuteo verb forms only ▼

FIGURE 10.30 Checkboxes used to select multiple items.

When writing checkbox text, you should follow these writing guidelines:

- The text should be specific enough for the user to understand what the "turn on" option actually turns on.
- The opposite action of not selecting the checkbox should be obvious.
- The text should be written in a positive manner.
- Options should be mutually exclusive and easily distinguishable from each other.
- The same structural writing format for each option in the list should be used.

Drop-down Menu Options

Drop-down menus, similar to radio buttons, are used when users can choose one item from a set of items. Drop-down menus are often a better choice when there are space constraints or when there are many options available. Drop-down menus are also a good choice when the items in the list are dynamic, changing based on other selections in the page, or may vary for different versions of the application.

In the following example, drop-down menus make it easy for users to see the current settings.

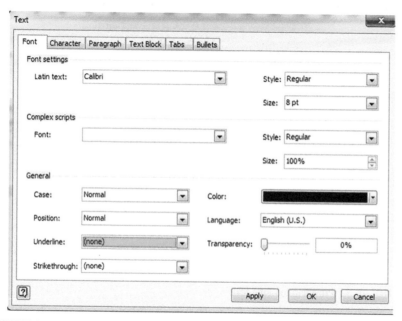

FIGURE 10.31 Example of drop-down menus.

The structural format of the text you use to write the options depends on the specific items in the list. The options in the following menu are very different from the options above. Both are valid and correct ways of writing drop-down menu items.

POP Download:
Learn more

1. Status: POP is enabled for all mail that has arrived since 4/17/08
   ○ Enable POP for all mail (even mail that's already been downloaded)
   ○ Enable POP for mail that arrives from now on
   ○ Disable POP

2. When messages are accessed with POP keep Gmail's copy in the Inbox ▼
   keep Gmail's copy in the Inbox
3. Configure your email client (e.g. Outlook, mark Gmail's copy as read
   Configuration instructions   archive Gmail's copy
                                             delete Gmail's copy

FIGURE 10.32 Ordering of items.

You also need to consider the ordering of the items. Ordering items alphabetically is a good method for long lists of items. For shorter lists, you may want to order items according to popularity—items you know most users select at the top (with the default value first in the list), and the least frequently selected items at the bottom.

Using Examples

Adding examples to your page is a good way to let users know what you expect them to enter in free-form text boxes. In this example, letting the users know the URL format and the picture formats supported will help them enter the URL correctly the first time, avoiding a validation error message.

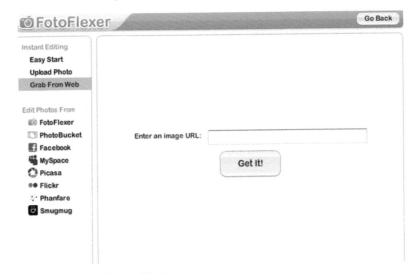

FIGURE 10.33 Providing too little text.

When users incorrectly enter a field, the error validation message should also provide an example. The user getting the following message after entering the URL incorrectly above may or may not be able to correct the error based on the message provided.

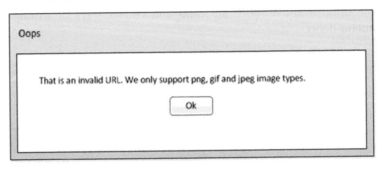

FIGURE 10.34 Example of a poorly written error.

Follow these general rules when writing examples:

- When possible, place the example text directly under the text box. The text box should indicate the number of accepted characters.
- Use a simple structure, such as: Example: www.mypictures/image.png
- Provide examples in validation error messages where needed.

Frames and Separator Lines

Frames and separator lines are useful for labeling and differentiating a set of controls from other controls in the page. The text you use in frames (also known as group boxes) and separator lines provide context for all the controls in the group. You can use sentence case, or title case; just remember to be consistent throughout the application.

Write titles that present concepts. For example, in the following picture, "Picture Sharpness" would probably be a better title for the first section rather than repeating the options, "Sharpen and Soften."

And be consistent in the ordering of the words. Using "Sharpen and Soften" for the title and then presenting them on the slider in reversed order will make the brain work harder.

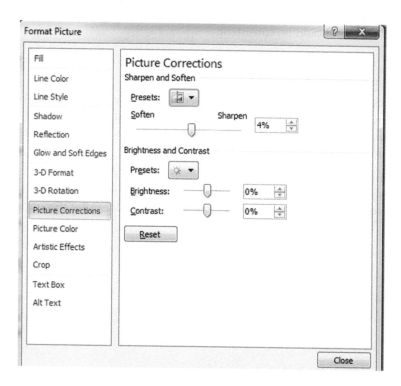

Separator text may be located above a group of controls, to the left of the controls, or in a frame around the controls. The text should be relevant to all the controls in the group.

Inbox type:	Classic ▾
Importance markers:	◉ Show markers - Show a marker (○) by messages marked as important. ○ No markers Gmail analyzes your new incoming messages to predict what's important, considering things like how you've treated similar messages in the past, how directly the message is addressed to you, and many other factors. Learn more
Filtered mail:	○ Override filters - Include important messages in the inbox that may have been filtered out. ◉ Don't override filters
	Save Changes Cancel

FIGURE 10.35 Using separators and grouping.

When writing separators and group labels, follow these guidelines:

- The text should present the main concept of the controls.
- The text should be kept simple, and words should be kept to a minimum.
- Structuring should be consistent.

Text Box Labels

Each text box or drop-down menu is accompanied by a label. This label can be above or next to the field to which it is relevant. When writing labels, remember to keep them succinct and focused on the object the user must either select or enter.

In addition, consider whether the imperative voice should be used. In the next example, most users will accept the default values and move on. If users were required to make a selection, you would consider using the imperative voice ("Select the envelope size:").

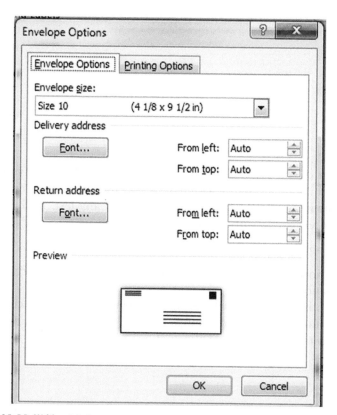

FIGURE 10.36 Writing labels.

Following these guidelines when writing textbox labels will help you write meaningful labels:

- Use noun phrases to help users scan the page.
- Keep labels short and concrete.
- Add information to a label only if it is relevant for users when they need to make a selection.

Hover Text

Hover text, often referred to as tooltips and info-tips, displays when the user hovers the pointer over an item without clicking. Hover text is useful for describing icons, adding explanations to interactive elements, and providing notifications.

The amount of text you include in hover text, or a tooltip, may vary. One or two words may be all that is required, or you may want to provide instructional content, as in the example above. As with any text, it's important to write hover text consistently for related items.

When writing hover text, follow these guidelines:

- If your hover text is a complete sentence, use sentence case with ending punctuation.
- If your hover text is a label or sentence fragment, do not use ending punctuation. For example, tooltips such as "Print options" and "Text tool" do not require ending punctuation.

Alt Text

Alt text is a term for alternative text or alt attribute. The alt text is used in HTML and XHTML pages for showing text for an image on a web page when images are turned off on a user's web browser, or when the screen reader is turned on.

The alt-text description displays in a small text box when users hover over the frame where an image is set to load. This is the text that screen readers will read to users who are using the screen reader feature.

FIGURE 10.37 Example of alt text on a logo.

When writing alt text, keep in mind that it defines the images for your users. As such, use words that describe the content of the image rather than the technical specifications or image parameters (for example, "Golden Gate Bridge," not "gif file of GGB").

Remember that the text should be short—only a few words—inasmuch as longer text strings result in auditory clutter for users relying on screen readers.

GENERAL TEXT GUIDELINES

Adhering to these general guidelines will help you provide text that follows the 4 A's of writing interactive content.

- Place the text close to the control if users need the information in order to complete an action. In this example, placing the instruction about how to include multiple file extensions is much more noticeable and therefore helpful when placed directly above the control rather than at the bottom of the page.

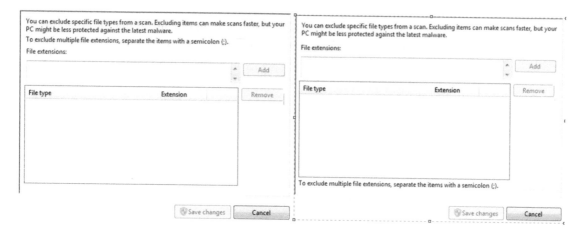

- Align controls to the right, with subordinate controls indented to the right.
- Use grouping (frames or line) separators, spacing, and alignment to show how controls are related to each other. Frames may also help you reduce the amount of text on the page by providing context for the group of controls.

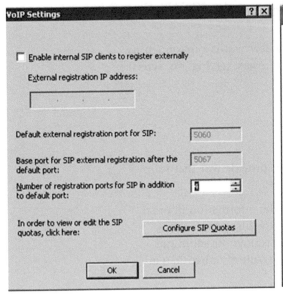
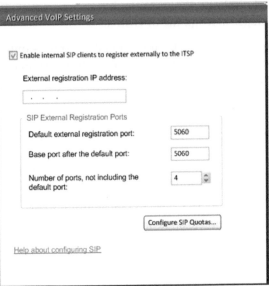

- Place notes and warnings above or alongside text if the information is relevant for making a selection or entering information in a field. In this example, the information in the warning is important for the user to understand when entering the user account details.

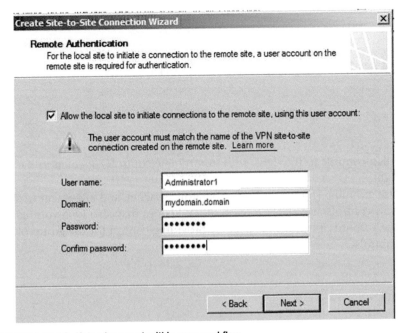

FIGURE 10.38 Note placement within user workflow.

- Place notes or warnings that contain information relevant for the page, but not necessary for making the current selection, toward the bottom of the page. In this example, the note provides information for actions they may want to take as a result of the selection made above.

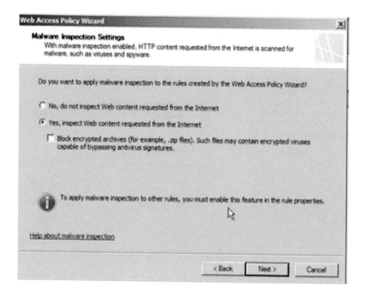

- Avoid redundant text. Too much text is difficult to read and understand. Try using help links to explain concepts if the page requires additional information. You can see below how the page on the right has less text but without reducing the important information.

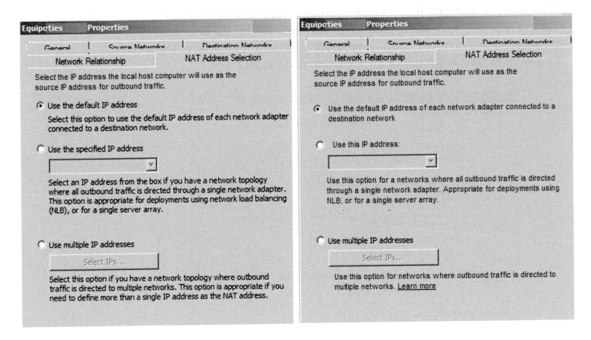

- When writing labels for ribbons or tooltips, use verbs or verb phrases whenever possible.

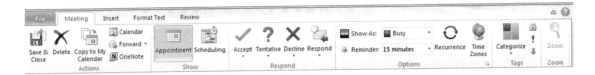

SUMMARY

In this chapter you learned about best practices for writing the information that appears within your application. Remember that your content must be easily available and should provide actionable information, be helpful, and be written at a level that is appropriate for your users.

Keep these principles in mind when writing your content:

- Callouts and help balloons are a good way to provide on-the-spot information.
- Callouts are also a good medium for guiding users through a series of tasks.
- Keep your user at the center of your text and use active voice whenever possible. But remember that passive voice is sometimes more appropriate for softening a message.
- Avoid generic titles. Instead, use titles that provide additional meaning to the page.
- Avoid redundant text. Too much text is difficult to read and understand.
- Avoid writing about the features. Instead write about the tasks.

CHAPTER 11

Writing for Diverse Audiences

INTRODUCTION

If your application is used by diverse audiences, you'll need to write in a way that is easily understood by nonnative English speakers and is easily accessible to users with disabilities. According to the U.S. Government Usability web site, approximately 8 percent of the user population has a disability that impacts the traditional use of a web site. When creating your style guidelines and writing your user interface text, it's important to remember that the information and textual cues within the user interface should be accessible to these users.

While the number of English speakers in the world is somewhere around 1.8 billion, only a small percentage actually speak English as a first language. In fact, more than 35 million adults in the United States are native speakers of a language other than English (U.S. Census Bureau, 2001). If your application is being translated into languages other than English, you will need to consider the impact of localization and globalization on your text.

This chapter describes the considerations and best practices for creating text that follows standard accessibility and text internationalization guidelines.

WRITING ACCESSIBLE CONTENT

Like web sites, software and web applications are considered accessible if they can be used as effectively by people with disabilities as by those without.[1]

---

[1]Keep in mind that "as effectively" is different from "as efficiently." In most cases it will be more cumbersome to use the accessibility features, but that should not prohibit users from completing the core tasks and use the application.

Generally, people with disabilities are grouped into four major categories:

- Visual disability: blindness, limited vision, color-blindness
- Hearing disability: hearing loss and deafness
- Physical disability: limited movement or fine motor control, difficulty or inability to use a mouse, slow response time
- Cognitive disability: cognitive limitations, learning disabilities, distractibility, inability to remember or focus on large amounts of information.

There are many ways the text and textual cues you provide in the user interface can help users with disabilities succeed in using your application. While accessibility guidelines vary from one country to another, most countries use the Web Content Accessibility Guidelines (WCAG) of the World Wide Web Consortium (W3C) as the basis for their accessibility criteria.

Writing Text that Meets WCAG2 Guidelines

Following WCAG2 guidelines as closely as possible will make content accessible to people with a wide range of disabilities and will also make your content easier to read for users in general. Following are the WCAG 2 guidelines you should be aware of when creating your text.

Perceivable

Provide **text alternatives** for nontext content.

Provide **captions and other alternatives** for multimedia.

Create content that can be **presented in different ways**, including by assistive technologies, without losing meaning.

Make it easier for users to **see and hear content**.

Operable

Make all functionality available from a **keyboard**.

Give users **enough time** to read and use content.

Do not use content that causes **seizures**.

Help users **navigate and find content**.

Understandable

Make text **readable and understandable**.

Make content appear and operate in **predictable** ways.

Help users **avoid and correct mistakes**.

Robust

Maximize **compatibility** with current and future user tools.

(Source:http://www.w3.org/WAI/WCAG20/glance).

In addition, in the United States, Section 508 of the U.S. Rehabilitation Act mandates that applications maintained by the federal government must be accessible to people with disabilities, and it prohibits federal agencies from buying, developing, maintaining, or using electronic and information technology that is inaccessible to people with disabilities.

The following sections describe how you can create text that meets WCAG 2 guidelines.

Creating Perceivable Content

Perceivable content is content that users can comprehend by relying on the provided visual, textual, or audible cues.

Augmenting Graphics with Text

When graphical elements are used to depict an object or action, the design of the metaphor provides helpful visual cues as to the related object or action. Using concrete metaphors helps users recognize the connection between the graphic and its meaning.

In the following sample, each graphical element is simple and concrete, and the accompanying text clarifies the meaning. This is a good example of how graphics and text should be used together to create perceivable content.

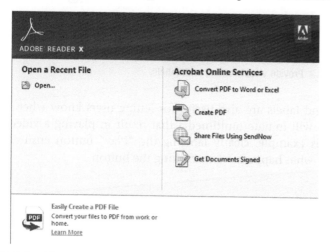

FIGURE 11.1 Providing concrete metaphors in icons.

Even the best designed graphics require effort to interpret, and you can't be sure users understand the intended metaphor. By providing text, such as tooltips or labels describing the graphical element (as in the picture above), you provide the required information and all your users will benefit from the additional input.

In the next sample, the chart is a valuable graphic for showing a visual representation of the information. The application does a good job of providing the information in other ways as well. Users can click on each area of the chart for a definition of each section, and users who cannot use the mouse can see the corresponding information in the table beneath it. This is a good example of how a graphical representation is combined with text to create perceivable content.

FIGURE 11.2 Provide visual content with labels.

Captions and labels are also useful for letting users know when clicking on an element will initiate multimedia that result in playing a video or animation. In this example, clearly labeling the "Play" button ensures that users understand what happens when clicking the button.

Watch the Guided Tour

FIGURE 11.3 Describe interactive elements.

Using Assistive Technologies

Assistive technologies also provide a means for helping users interact with your application by using alternative interaction mechanisms. When writing instructions and text strings, it's important for you to understand how assistive technologies are designed to let your users view, hear, and interact with your content.

Screen Readers

A screen reader is a software application that attempts to recognize and interpret the text and visual elements displayed on the page. The interpreted text is provided to the user via sound (e.g., text-to-speech) or another output device (e.g., Braille Output Reader).

Screen readers are useful for anyone who has difficulties reading the interface text due to visual or other reading impairments, and most operating systems have screen reader assistive technologies built into the system.

FIGURE 11.4 Windows Built-In Screen Reader Technology.

You can make it easier for users to see and hear content by following these simple guidelines:

- When creating your text, keep in mind that large chunks of text do not read well. Use short, concise sentences and phrasing—which is good practice under any circumstances.
- Structure your content to facilitate the good vocalization. Grouping controls either in a frame or with a separator will make it easier for users to understand the page structure and context of your options.
- Use consistent text structuring such as punctuation and phrasing.
- Use concrete and consistent terminology to describe concepts and actions—for example, Turn on/Turn off, Allow/Deny, Increase/Decrease.
- Include units of measure in the main text strings. Screen readers generally move down to the next line of text after an input field. This means that any text appearing after the field will be missed. In the example on the left, users will have no way of knowing that the input field relates to minutes.

Incorrect	Better
Signal an alert after [ ] minutes	Signal an alert after (minutes): [ ]
	Signal an alert after this number of minutes: [ ]
Stop the alert automatically after: [ ] times	Number of times the alert should signal: [ ]
	Stop the alert after it signals this number of times: [ ]

Creating Operable Content

Operable content ensures that uses with limited movement are able to interact successfully with your application. At the most basic level, this means avoiding the use of flashing text or text that moves on the page, without a clear way for users to stop the movement.

One common interaction method for users unable to manipulate a mouse or other pointing device is to use keyboard strokes (hotkeys) instead.

Making Functionality Available from the Keyboard

Users who find it difficult to manipulate a mouse or other pointing device may rely on keyboard strokes or other input devices to select options and enter data. These users should be able to move through your pages in two ways:

- Using a single keystroke (i.e., tab) or movement to move linearly through the options and fields in the page
- Using hotkeys and keyboard strokes to move to specific options and fields

With single keystroke or other touch apparatus used for this purpose, you have little to do other than make sure the cursor moves in the right direction and moves directly from one field to the next, without skipping around the page. When using the keyboard, this movement is generated using the Tab key. For some controls, the arrow keys or other keystrokes may be used in combination with the Tab key. In this example, the user clicks Tab to move through the options and then uses the up and down arrow keys to control the location of the slider.

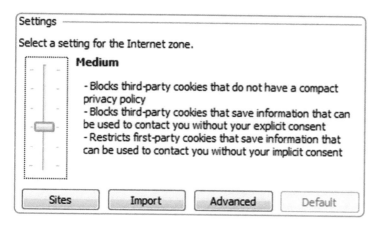

Hotkeys allow users to move through the pages of your application using the Alt key combined with a keystroke. The hotkey letters appear underlined in the text string, and while this is straightforward, there are some basic guidelines you should follow to make it easier for your users.

- Remember that some keys are reserved for standard button actions—A for Apply, C for Cancel, and Enter for OK. Always use these hotkeys consistently throughout your application.
- When possible, use key letters that match the related action. Using B for Block or D for Delete makes more sense than using any other letter within the text string.

This is a good example of how hotkeys are matched to the associated actions.

FIGURE 11.5 Associated hotkeys.

■ Use key letters that are highly visible. The first letter in a word is easier to find than a letter appearing in the middle of a word. Round letters provide a larger surface for underlining. Letters such as i and l do not provide enough width for the underline to be easily visible. In the following example the l in the second option is the hot key; the underline is difficult to see, especially on higher resolution monitors.

FIGURE 11.6 Key letters should be visible.

And in this next example, it is difficult to discern which hotkey is underlined for the first checkbox.

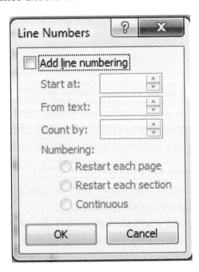

- Avoid using letters that dip below the text line, such as g and j. The underline is difficult to discern from the dip of the letter. In the following example, the first hotkey is the letter g, and the underline is barely visible.

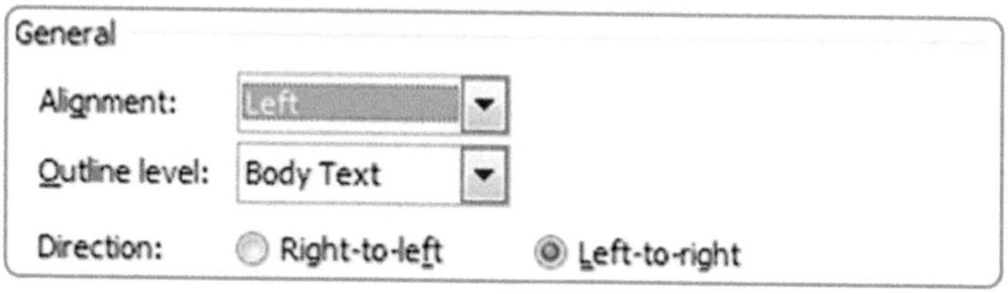

FIGURE 11.7 Avoid letters dipping below the line.

Links navigating to another page or opening a new page should be clearly written, visible, and easily accessible. The links in the page are clearly written, letting the user know the actions to expect.

FIGURE 11.8 Examples of Navigation links.

Creating Understandable Content

Hopefully, your text is understandable not just for users with special needs, but for all your users. Here are some simple guidelines that will help you structure your content to facilitate reading and create text that is more easily understood by people who may have limited reading or comprehension problems in particular, and by all your users.

- Use concise, common words. Use a simpler word where one exists.
- Group related controls together in a frame or by using separators.
- Use consistent text structuring such as punctuation and phrasing.
- Use uniform spacing and follow indentation rules so that users can easily see which controls have dependencies and which do not.
- Use the same words for like concepts.
- Use your text-writing guidelines consistently across pages and features.

Creating Robust Content

Remember that users are interacting with your content on a variety of platforms and devices. The information you provide and the text cues in your pages should provide a positive, easy to understand experience across platforms and devices.

- Write commands, instructions, and labels that are appropriate for different input mechanisms and interfaces (i.e., touch, speech recognition, and mouse-driven applications). Is the user clicking or selecting? Swiping or tapping? Unless you are sure how users are interacting with your application, use commands that are generic, such as "Select" or "Choose."
- Remember that different devices have varying screen sizes and that users may change the font size and resolution for their specific visual needs. Keep text and labels to a minimum to avoid the need to scroll on different-sized screens.

WRITING FOR INTERNATIONAL AUDIENCES

Whether your application is sold in a box or downloaded from the Internet, you will need to consider ways to make your content easy to read and understand for users who are not native English speakers. The overall term to describe this process is *internationalization*. Creating an internationalized product also includes localization and globalization processes.

- *Internationalization* is the process of designing an application so that it can be adapted for potential use anywhere in the world. (Microsoft refers to this as "world-ready.")
- *Localization* is the process of adapting the application for a specific location or region other than the one for which the application was originally developed. This includes translating the text strings and messages within the application as well as modifying other textual cues on the page.
- *Globalization* is the process of creating an application that is suitable across cultures and regions.

You can think of it this way: Internationalization makes sure users can select the date format for their locale, and localization assures the names of the days and months are translated correctly, while globalization assures that the calendar adheres to cultural preferences such as displaying the appropriate holidays for that locale on the calendar.

The infrastructure required for internationalization is built into the software design by the developers. However, providing the right language and cultural references within the application generally falls on the writer.

Considerations for Internationalization

Internationalization implies that users can view the application in the native language of their locale and that the application will display and accept input in the formats appropriate to that locale. In particular, displays and input should be formatted appropriately for objects such as date, time, number, and currency, which are based on the linguistic and cultural preferences of each locale. Because internationalization is built into the product design, it is generally done once during the product development cycle.

Even a simple field, such as entering a short date, can have many variations depending on locale, with some countries using different delimiters (e.g., DD/MM/YY and DD-MM-YY) , while others use different ordering (e.g., YY/MM/DD and MM/DD/YY and formats YYYY/MM/DD or YY.MM.DD. In addition, some locales use leading zeros, while others do not (e.g., 05 or 5). You cannot assume that everyone will understand 04/06/02 to mean the same date.

While a long date may be easier to understand, different countries and regions have different ways of spelling out dates. For your application to be world-ready, it should allow the user to select the date and time formatting for their locale.

The following examples show how dates, times, and date preferences are shown for the United States and Mexico.

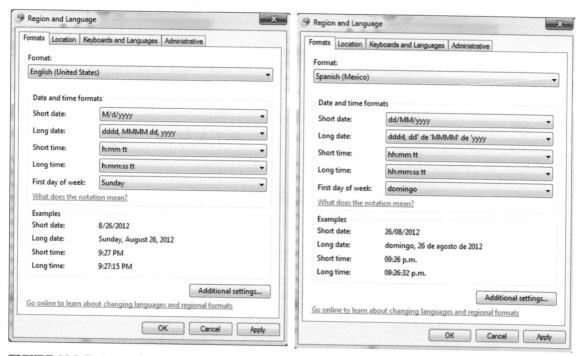

FIGURE 11.9 Each locale has its own settings.

Considerations for Localization

Localization and globalization processes are implemented and verified as needed throughout the product life cycle. While the main component of localization is the translation of the text strings, there are other considerations regarding the localization of an application.

If your strings are translated into a variety of languages, you can expect words or strings in some languages to be at least 30 percent longer than the equivalent term in English. When writing your text and deciding how it appears in the page, you should allow up to 30 percent extra spacing for each text string appearing in your user interface.

English	German	Dutch
Apply	Anwenden	van toepassing zijn
Click to continue	Klicken Sie weiter	Klik om verder te gaan
Edit settings	Einstellungen bearbeiten	Instellingen bewerken

Creating guidelines and a localization checklist helps you create text that is ready and easier to translate and localize when the time arises. And if your application is not translated, but will be used by diverse audiences, these guidelines will help ensure that all your users find your text easy to understand. Following are basic guidelines you should follow when defining your rules and writing your text:

Language Considerations

■ Decide which version of English you're using as the primary language. Then use the appropriate spellings and wording for the selected version. Don't use both American English and British English spelling and terms (e.g., color versus colour).

■ Write for clarity, using simple English and simple words. Remember that even simple words can be misinterpreted if they have double meanings or could be interpreted in different ways.

Incorrect	Correct
Select whether you want . . .	Select if you want . . .
Follow this procedure:	Follow these steps:
Once you complete this step . . .	After completing this step . . .
In other words . . .	(This one should never be used; if you have to explain your text, it probably needs to be rewritten)

- Avoid complex sentences and large blocks of text.
- Languages have varying punctuation rules. Keep in mind that capitalization, exclamation marks, hyphens, question marks, and quotation marks are language dependent.

English	Spanish	French
Do you want to save this image?	¿Quieres guardar esta imagen?	Voulez-vous sauvegarder l'image?
Warning!	¡Advertencia!	Attention!

Avoid using (s) or /s to indicate plural. Different languages have different plural forms, and these conventions will not translate well. It may be easier to change the way the text is presented if you have to accommodate plurals.

Incorrect	Correct
Select the image(s)	Select the images:
Enter the date/s	Enter the dates:
Found N item(s)	Items found: N

Words and Values Using Numerals

- Always indicate the correct format for entering numbers. Some countries use a dot as a decimal separator, while others use a comma (1.000 or 1,000).
- If users must enter a time, make sure the format for entering the time is clear. Not all users understand and use the same formatting to indicate time, and there are different formats for indicating a.m. and p.m. Also keep in mind that users are located in varying time zones.
- If users must enter a date, make sure the correct format is provided and that the interface provides guidance. Having the user select the day, month, and year from a drop-down list or calendar will help avoid any confusion.
- If users must enter contact details such as addresses, keep in mind that not all countries have zip codes, and that the format of the address may vary based on location.
- If users must enter phone numbers, remember that phone number formats and country codes vary in length and in the number of digits. Allow for these differences, and provide examples as needed for international phone numbers. For example, a U.S. phone number may be presented in any number of ways, depending on the locale of the person making the call.

Number	Format
555–1212	Local phone
(541) 555–1212	Domestic
+1-541-555-1212	International
1-541-555-1212	Dialed in the United States
001-541-555-1212	Dialed from Germany
191 541 555-1212	Dialed from France

■ Provide examples and verification to prevent errors.

Considerations for Globalization

Following globalization guidelines helps ensure that your content matches the cultural preferences of your users. This is important for improving the overall user experience, and it also helps make your customers feel comfortable using your application.

Here are some simple guidelines you can follow for creating content that is globalized for your users:

■ Colors can have different meanings in different cultures. Before using colored text and placing text on colored backgrounds, research how the colors are perceived in the cultures of your target users. For example, in the following picture, the application uses green for accenting text and for text background colors. This is appropriate use of color since green is associated with money for the target audience (United States). However, if the application was intended for a global audience, green could be problematic as it indicates infidelity or exorcism in China and corruption in North Africa.

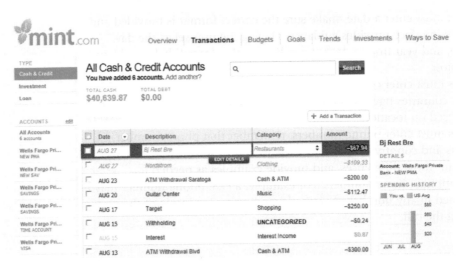

- If your application includes maps or mentions geographical locations, ensure that any disputed territories or areas are dealt with in a way that is sensitive to your users. Keep in mind that borders also change with time, so it's best to avoid using border-specific details in your descriptions and text.
- Ensure that the titles you provide for areas, regions, dignitaries, or religious leaders are the acceptable and preferred names for the locale. Remember that names of locales and titles of dignitaries change with time. Avoid using time-specific information in your descriptions and examples.
- Provide generic examples of names and companies in examples. Using a real company from a specific local in your examples may insult or upset users in another locale. You can avoid this by using generic terms such as "my company" or make up a company name and use it throughout your samples.
- If your users must enter an identity number (such as social security, passport, or driver's license), make sure your application accepts the format for the locale of the user. While the United States generally accepts a social security number for identifying its citizens, not all locales have similarly formatted forms of identification.
- Each country has its own way of writing currencies. These variations include the currency symbol and its position, the formats used to show positive or negative amounts, and the punctuation separating numbers (e.g., placement and usage of dot and comma). Allow for these differences in the way currency values are displayed and entered, and specify the currency being shown with the symbol and universally accepted acronym.

In the next samples, you can see the different formats for currency shown in U.S. dollars and German euros.

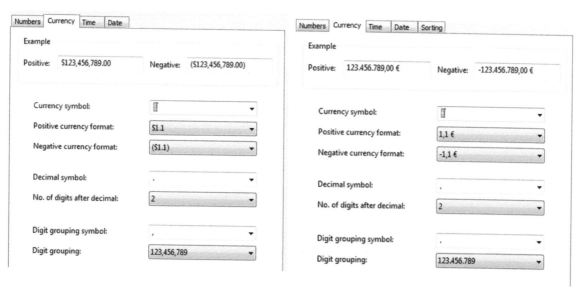

When your interface provides a unit of measure, remember that most countries use the metric system. Always provide the accurate unit of measure as specified by the International System of Units guidelines for unit measurements and symbols. Common units and their corresponding symbols are shown in the table.

Quantity	Unit	Symbol
Length, width, distance, thickness, girth, etc.	millimeter	mm
	centimeter	cm
	meter	m
	kilometer	km
Mass ("weight")*	milligram	mg
	gram	g
	kilogram	kg
Time	second	s
	minute	min
	hour	hr
Temperature	degree Celsius	°C
	degree Fahrenheit	°F

- Unit symbols are case-sensitive. Changing the upper- and lowercase letters changes the meaning of the unit.
- Units do not have plural forms and should not have a plural "s" at the end (e.g., 1 kg, 2 kg, etc.).
- Units are not abbreviations; they are symbols. So, there's no period after a unit symbol (unless it happens to fall at the end of a sentence).

SUMMARY

In this chapter you learned how to make your content easily accessible to diverse audiences, such as people with disabilities, and to people living in different locales.

- Your content should be accessible to users with visual, hearing, physical, and cognitive disabilities.
- Following the WCAG2 guidelines will help you create content that is accessible to people with a wide range of disabilities.
- Content should be perceivable, operable, understandable, and robust.
- Assistive technologies help users interact with your application.
- Users who cannot manipulate a mouse or pointing device rely on hotkeys. Use hotkeys that are meaningful and easily noticed.
- Help users understand content by grouping objects and using concise language. Your information should be easy to read on a variety of devices.
- If your application will be used by people in varying locales, consider internationalization, localization, and globalization issues when designing and writing your content.

Evaluation

Regardless of how well you've planned, designed, written, and created the information experience, there will always be ways to improve the information. At best, these are little refinements. At worst, a vital piece of information is missing or inaccurate, causing users to stumble or fail. For this reason, validating the information experience is a vital step in the process. Validating the information by reviewing it with the team is the first step. But to understand the effectiveness of your information, and of the information experience as a whole, the best method is to observe users who are part of your target audience interact with your application, relying on the information you've provided.

This section describes ways for you to validate the information experience and shows how to prioritize issues as they arise.

CHAPTER 12

Evaluating Your Information Experience

INTRODUCTION

On my first day on the job as an information designer, I was given the task of reviewing the user interface text for an educational software product. I sat in front of the application, and the first page I came across had this sentence across the top:

At first glance, the sentence appeared to be just fine; it contained no grammatical errors or spelling mistakes. Yet, something about it made me stop and think about it. It just didn't feel right—and that's when I realized that even the most talented writer makes mistakes and that text reviews are crucial for ensuring the success of the information experience.

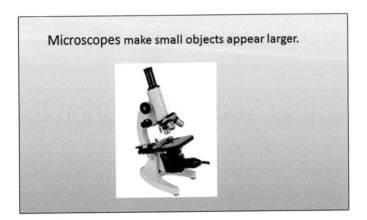

In the example of the microscope, only a minor change was required to fix the sentence, making it accurate.

Depending on the complexity of your application, of each feature or page in your application, and of the text, your pages may require deeper evaluations and revisions throughout the writing process. This chapter describes methods you can use to gather the information for evaluating your text and shows how you can use the information to improve the information experience of your application.

WHAT ARE YOU REVIEWING FOR?

When you work on an application, you become familiar with the nuances and attributes of the user interface. But even the best written block of text, widget string, or description can be surprisingly confusing to your audience, which is seeing the information for the first time. To ensure that your text provides the right information and is easily understood by your users, you will need to review and evaluate the text—not just string by string, but within the context of the user tasks and at each step in the user workflows.

The type and depth of your text reviews are tied directly to your application milestones. The sooner you start getting feedback, the better chance you have of providing a better information experience.

Verifying the information experience requires more than checking that your pages of text are accurate and well written. The information must also provide the right level of details, as well as the time and place when the user needs it.

Evaluating your information experience means checking that following your writing guidelines and the principles of writing for interaction have resulted in providing the right information experience.

Accuracy

First and foremost, it's crucial to ensure that the text in your application is correct, accurate, and honest, and written in a way that gives users confidence in your application. Imagine the effect that even a small miscommunication can have in a networking application where the smallest details are central for properly configuring an application and any inaccuracies in the information can cause a misconfiguration. Inaccurate text can result in users wasting hours, or even days, trying to understand why the application is not working, or why they are having problems with their computer or network configuration. Not only will users think twice about using your product, you could even find your company liable for damages.

Validating the accuracy of your text includes thinking about these attributes:

Are you using the right terms? If there are standard industry terms available for features, options, and information in your application, verify that the terms you use, and the way you use them, are accurate and easy to understand. Also, if you created new terms specific to the features in your application, you'll want to ensure that they are easily understood and make sense to your users.

Is the information honest? Your users expect that the information and text displayed in the user interface, and the recommendations you make, will help them make the right decisions and stop them from making errors. Not only are you considered an authority about the subject, but also you are their expert about the features and functionality of your application. Creating trust with your users requires that you are honest about what the application or features provide, and where needed, the implications of selecting different options.

Clarity and Conciseness

When reading your text, it's important to remember that users are trying to do something—either decide what they want to do next, complete a task, or learn about a concept. If users have to read and reread text several times to understand it, then the text is lacking in clarity. If users wonder why the text is provided, then it may be irrelevant and unnecessary. Remember that your text should provide as much information as needed, in as few words as possible. It should also be written in a way that allows users to scan for pertinent information.

When evaluating your text for clarity and conciseness, you'll want to answer these questions:

- *Is the text easily understood?* Users should be able to read a text string, sentence, or paragraph one time to understand its message. If the user must read the text several times to understand the concepts, or how the text relates to the options in the page, your text is not written in a way that is understandable.
- *Is there redundant text?* Remember that information should be easy to scan. This means that long blocks of text and lengthy explanations should be cut down as much as possible. Verify that each word, sentence, or paragraph adds meaning to the page and that you are not repeating yourself. Words that should never be found in the user interface are "In other words." If you need to repeat yourself, then the information isn't written properly.
- *Is the text necessary?* Sometimes it's difficult to avoid the desire to tell the user everything about a feature or option. This is particularly a problem when the project manager or developer is excited about his or her feature and wants to explain how it works. Most users don't need to understand how an algorithm is constructed. Nor do they want a sales pitch embedded in a dialog box. When evaluating the text, you may need to make some difficult decisions about what text to remove and what text is essential. Most important, if the text does not help the user make a selection, complete a task, or move through a workflow, then it is probably not necessary within the user interface and should be removed.

Look at the next example. What information is necessary, and what could be removed? The paragraphs in the middle are unnecessary and create a confusing page. These should be removed. And the other text strings can be reduced.

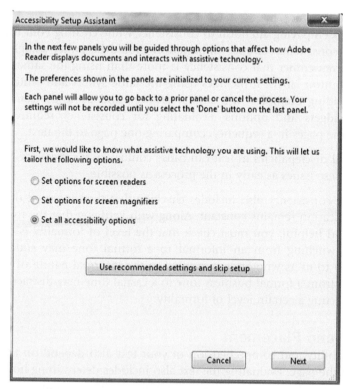

FIGURE 12.1 Example of a page with extraneous text.

Removing the extraneous text improves the readability of the page.

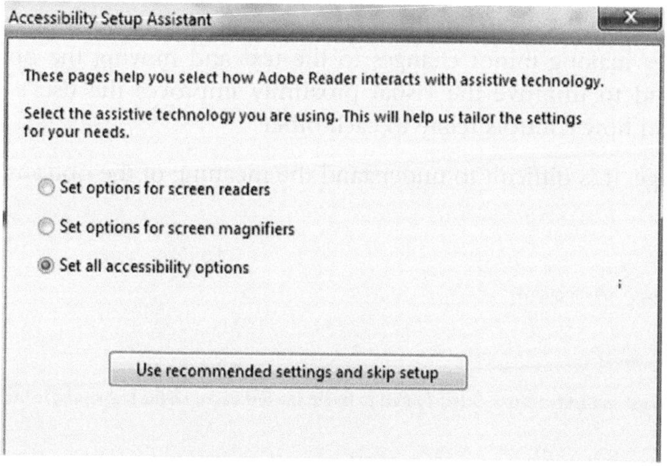

FIGURE 12.2 Page with text reduced to improve readability.

Consistency

If you've been paying attention to consistency while creating your text, evaluating the consistency of your information should be rather straightforward. However, remember that consistency is more than using the same terminology and button labels. It includes using the same syntax and sentence structure, providing examples in a similar fashion, and using the same text for similar widgets and options. Evaluating for consistency requires clicking through the pages in a sequence, comparing one page to the next.

Even small discrepancies in text can cause confusion; it's therefore helpful to identify these issues as early in the process as possible.

Validating consistency also includes checking that the tone used throughout your application remains constant. Along with verifying that the tone is supportive and helpful, you must check that the level of formality is consistent as well. Switching from an informal to a formal tone may suddenly feel unfriendly to users who are accustomed to the informal nature of your text. Changing from a formal business tone to a casual tone may distract or annoy users expecting a certain level of formality.

Layout and Placement

The readability and comprehension of your text also depend on the overall layout of the page. Evaluating the text also includes determining how the layout of the page helps or hinders the user's ability to understand the text.

Evaluating the page layout includes verifying that the placement of the text on the page matches the expected information flow and that the way controls are grouped and placed on the page, and the proximity between text elements, all help users understand the content provided in the page. Sometimes making minor changes to the text and moving the options and text around to improve the visual proximity improves the user's ability to understand how controls relate to each other.

In this page, it is difficult to understand the meaning of the options.

Right to Left

Arrange panes left to right for right to left languages
Define the direction of your views:
- Left to Right
- Right to Left

Define the global text direction of strings and edit controls. Select context to layout the text based on the first strong left to right or right to left character detected:
- Left to Right
- Context
- Right to Left

Adding a noun to the title of the page helps keep the settings in context. Moving the explanations closer to the option to which it is relevant also improves the overall information flow in the page.

Right to Left Languages

☐ Arrange panes left to right for right to left languages
Define the direction of your views:
◉ Left to Right
○ Right to Left
Define the global text direction of strings and edit controls:
○ Left to Right
◉ Context Select Context to layout the text based on the first strong left to right or right to left character detected
○ Right to Left

Discoverability

Even the most important and well-written text string or piece of information is only useful if it can be seen. When evaluating your text, remember to validate and ensure that important information is easy to find. In particular, ensure that any warnings or information relevant to a specific option is within proximity of that option, at the time the user needs to read it.

In a web application, you'll need to verify that the most important information is available at the top of the page. If users must scroll to see a pertinent piece of text, there is a good chance they will miss it.

In Section 3, we looked at heat maps to show how users scan text. Verifying where text appears on different-size monitors will help you determine whether information is placed too far down on the page.

PLANNING YOUR EVALUATION STRATEGY

In a perfect world, you would evaluate each text string, button label, and the information experience until you were sure it's perfect. In reality, software teams generally don't have the time and bandwidth to continuously update the user interface, moving and changing text strings around. By scheduling text reviews and evaluations into the product schedule, you can help ensure that the information experience is positive and helpful and if not perfect, then pretty close to perfect!

Creating a Schedule

When defining your writing guidelines and creating your text, you'll need to schedule review milestones into your application development milestones. This will allow you to gather feedback at regular intervals, update the text based on the input, and then verify the updated text. In general, your review and validation dates should coincide with the code check in and build schedule, and build release dates of the application development cycle.

If you are working in an agile development process, you may have an initial release and then incremental updates and versions throughout the life cycle of the application. This allows you more flexibility to update text and improve the information experience throughout the life cycle of the product.

If your application is released in a box, however, you may have one or two preliminary versions before the release. Any improvements to the text must be implemented much earlier in the product cycle, often weeks or months before the application release date. If your product is being translated for a release, you may find that any improvements and fixes to the information and content provided in the user interface are required much earlier in the development cycle than you would expect.

Creating a schedule and process that the team agrees upon ahead of time will help you understand the deadlines and milestones for getting your text reviewed and implemented.

The evaluation methods you use will depend on the amount of time and resources you have. While you may not be able to apply all these methods for each feature and option, you should at least find time to evaluate your information experience in one or more of these ways.

Define Your Golden Pages

In Section 3, when discussing your writing strategy, we looked at how you can prioritize the pages in your application by categorizing them as gold, silver and bronze:

- Gold: Core to the application. High visibility, high impact.
- Silver: Core to the secondary features and scenarios. High-medium visibility and impact.
- Bronze: Low visibility, noncore feature, low impact.

When reviewing the information experience, you'll want to check out those priorities again. New features may have been added, and initial feedback from the team may give cause to make changes.

As you plan your evaluation schedule and methods, you will want to make sure all the "gold" pages are given the highest priority. Gold pages generally include welcome pages, landing pages, getting started wizards, and pages used for configuring key features. Silver pages generally include options and dialogs that many people will use, but less than 80 percent. Bronze options affect around 20 percent of your users.

Providing Recommendations

Depending on how your team decides to deal with issues discovered during the information reviews, you may need to open bugs, or create a list of issues. Each issue you discover should be accompanied by a recommendation on how to improve the text or fix the issues that were discovered, based on careful analysis of the feedback. Stating the problem and providing a thoughtful recommendation will expedite the process and result in a better user experience.

In a perfect world, every text issue you identify which negatively affects the information and user experience would be fixed. However, with tight deadlines and limited resources, you may find that you need to make choices as to which issues get fixed and which are left for another release.

Creating content and text bug triage guidelines helps the team decide which issues are critical and which can be postponed. Here is a sample of how guidelines may be created to determine which issues must be fixed and which can wait until resources become available.

Priority 0 (highest)	Priority 1 (high)	Priority 2 (medium)	Priority 2 (low)
Current implementation will likely result in a	Inaccurate or incomplete text results in a core feature being	Current text does not adhere to the guidelines. Customers	Little or no impact

Continued...

Continued

Priority 0 (highest)	Priority 1 (high)	Priority 2 (medium)	Priority 2 (low)
call to customer support. Blocks users from configuring or using the feature. Inaccurate information results in a misconfiguration or data loss. Embarrassment to the company.	hard to configure or use. May result in misconfiguration of the feature. Current implementation results in misinterpretation of data (incomplete or missing data).	will be aware or annoyed by inconsistencies. Current text results in data being difficult to interpret. Nonintuitive or incomplete text of a noncore feature results in the feature being difficult to configure.	to the user.

The table is useful for describing and understanding the impact of the issues you will discover while evaluating your information. When deciding what issues have priority and must be fixed, keep in mind that text issues for core features—the ones that that everyone will come across—are higher priority than features that are not central to the application.

Looking at the next screen, let's see how you might explain the issue to the team, either in a bug or using whatever means your team implements to track and fix problems identified in the user interface:

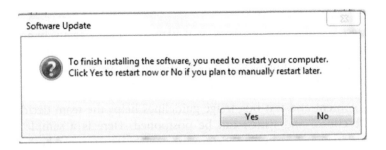

Issue	Recommendation
The second sentence does not provide the appropriate options for the action.	Change the sentence or update the buttons.

Although this recommendation provides enough information for someone to understand the problem, it does not provide the information required to fix the problem.

A better recommendation would look something like this:

RECOMMENDATION

Change the sentence to: Do you want to restart the application now? If you click No, you will need to restart the application manually later.

EVALUATION METHODS

Chances are that your team has a code review process in place for the developers and a spec review process for product managers to present feature specification. Before any code is released, there is a testing (QA) process in place to verify that the code meets a set of standards. For the same reasons, information experience and text reviews are crucial to ensuring the quality of your application.

Many of the evaluation methods applicable for verifying your information experience are used for testing usability. Since the user experience and information experience are so closely tied together, testing the usability of the user experience elicits insights and feedback about the information experience. In the same way, evaluating and testing your information experience will provide valuable insights into the overall usability of your application. For this reason, it's good practice to plan the evaluations with the user interface designer, product manager, or other stakeholders involved in designing the application. Sometimes adding text to the page is a good, quick fix for a usability issue. Sometimes the design of a feature requires a bigger fix than additional text can provide. Working hand in hand with the designer or feature owner will help create an information and user experience that melds together.

Team Reviews

Team reviews of the code not only improve the quality of the product, but also provide a chance for the feature stakeholders to voice concern, provide input, and agree on designs. For all these reasons, it's good practice to have a formal team review of the information experience and text strings accompanying each feature. Getting input from the team helps ensure that the text is accurate, and that the proposed flow of information and matches the workflow of the design. At the same time, you may identify areas within a workflow that require more text and areas where links to help topics would be helpful.

When looking at the text and layout, it's important that the stakeholders agree on the resources and schedule required for building the information.

Planning the Team Review

Before you show your content to a team of coworkers, it's a good idea to go over your suggestions with someone who is familiar with the feature. This will give you a chance to see how someone else reacts to the information flow and text, and also lets you ensure the correctness and accuracy of your information before showing it to a group.

When you are ready for the review, following these next steps will help you keep the review focused and let you obtain the feedback you need.

1. Prepare a presentation with the pages for review. You can copy the pages into a file, such as Visio or PowerPoint, or you may be able to use the actual screens.
2. Send copies of the presentation (or pages) to the relevant members of the team (i.e., the feature owner, programmer, designer, tester, and technical writer). Ask for their suggestions before the meeting so that you can address any questions or concerns that may arise ahead of time.
3. Send out the invitation for the review meeting. The number of people you invite and the exact makeup of participants in the meeting, depend on the structure of your team.

At the Review

1. At the meeting present the ideas, describing the user workflow. Give the team time to read the text and comment.
2. Take notes so that you remember what was said. You may not agree with all the comments or suggestions, but you should record them.
3. At the end of the meeting clarify the main issues and define the next steps.

After the Review

- After the meeting send out a summary of the comments, suggestions, and concerns. Include any action items or milestones that were decided on at the meeting. You don't have to provide suggestions and alternatives to each issue in the summary.
- Update and fix the information based on the feedback. If you have a presentation, update the text strings and send it back out to the team.

Some members of the team may have strong opinions as to how information should be presented and what text should be included. It's important to accept all suggestions in a positive way.

Heuristic Evaluations

Traditionally, heuristic evaluations are a quick and informal way to find usability issues by gathering feedback from usability experts about the user interface—such as layout, user interaction, and workflow. The same techniques can be used for evaluating and validating the information experience within the application. In fact, because the user experience and information experience are so closely linked, checking one aspect of the application leads to identifying issues in the other.

All you need for a heuristic evaluation is a mockup of the page or pages you are evaluating. The screens can be drawn on paper, in a working prototype, or coded, which makes this an effective and low-cost method for gathering feedback throughout the development cycle of the application.

The experts you recruit for your heuristic evaluations are not necessarily usability experts but should have some level of expertise with the subject matter or technology required to use your application. If you have a customer support team, or anyone who works directly with customers, you may want to start there. Later on in the development phase, you may want to show your text to sample users from your target user groups.

Planning the Heuristic Evaluation

While each evaluation provides new insights, you can keep the sample quite small and still gather a large amount of viable information. Generally, using three to five good, experienced participants results in discovering 80 to 90 percent of the issues. After that number, the return on investment drops significantly.

Following these next steps will help you gather valuable information:

1. Prepare the mockups of your pages. You can use a graphics program, or draw the mockups on paper.
2. Recruit your experts. Finding participants with a range of experience levels will provide a broader range of useful feedback and insights.
3. Create a list of five to ten heuristics you want to assess. For example, your heuristics may include:
   - Is the terminology correct?
   - Is the information in the right location?
   - Does the placement of the information match the user workflow?
   - Do users understand the labels?
   - Do users understand what to do next?
   - Is the outcome of a selection obvious?
   - Is the right level of information provided?

Create a list of tasks you want participants to complete. While interaction may not be possible when using paper mockups, your participants should be able to tell you how they think a specific task would be completed based on the pages they are looking at.

Running the Heuristic Evaluation

After you have created your mockups, and have decided what feedback you are looking for, it's time to invite the participants. You will want to take notes throughout the session, so if possible, invite a co-worker to sit in on the session with you so that you don't miss anything. Better yet, ask that person to take notes for you. You may even want to tape the session.

1. Make sure that the atmosphere is friendly and inviting, and that you are all set up when the participants arrive. Also, if the participants are not from your company, you will want them to sign a nondisclosure agreement. Schedule 1 to 2 hours per session, allowing time to greet the participants and debrief them after the session.

2. Explain to the participants the overall purpose of the application and of the features they are evaluating. Give them the list of heuristics so that they understand the level of feedback you are looking for. And urge them to think out loud throughout the session.

3. Have the participants take a few minutes to simply look at the page and tell you what they would do first on the page. This lets you know what catches their eye on first glance.

4. Using your tasks as a guide, ask the participants to tell you how they would complete a specific task using the information and options provided. Ask specific questions about what each option is used for and how they would interact with the available options and features. Avoid the tendency to overexplain, or disagree with a suggestion. Just note all issues and keep moving through the tasks.

5. Remember to use your list of heuristics to ask questions and elicit feedback from the participants. Ask them about the terms in the interface and what actions they will take based on the information provided.

6. After going through all the tasks, spend a few minutes talking to the participants about the overall experience. Give them a chance to offer suggestions based on their knowledge and experience. You don't have to agree, but note their suggestions and be gracious about any criticism.

After the Evaluation

1. Review the feedback from all the evaluations to look for similarities and differences. Based on your analysis of the participants' comments and the

trends you discovered, decide how you can improve the terminology, information flow, text, labels, and so on.

2. Make the fixes accordingly. This may require you to meet with your product team or UX designer to find ways to change the information flow or to deal with any other issues that came up during the evaluations.

Because heuristic evaluations are a quick and an inexpensive method for gathering rich feedback, you can use this method throughout the life cycle of the application, as new features are added and legacy features are revised.

Feature Walkthroughs

Similar to heuristic evaluations, feature walkthroughs are an inexpensive way to gather viable feedback and insights from a small number of sample users. Feature walkthroughs let you observe how users complete a task or workflow required to configure an entire feature or set of features. This helps you decide whether the information encountered along the way, and the text used for each widget, button, label, and the like, provide the right content when and where it is most useful.

Ideally, your walkthrough participants will match the knowledge levels and characteristics of your target users. However, even teammates who are not involved in the design of that particular part of the user experience can provide useful information—provided you keep in mind the differences between them and your target users. Although at some level some of your coworkers may also fall into your target group, they are probably more computer savvy than typical users.

Depending on where you are in the writing and development process, you will need to decide how you are testing the feature; if the feature is not already coded, you may need to create a prototype or presentation. This will require some time upfront to prepare, and it could limit the user's activities, but it will not adversely impact the results of the walkthrough.

Planning the Feature Walkthrough

Similar to other methods described earlier, the first task is to decide on the activities the user is going to complete. It's generally a good idea to work together with the feature owner or designer to plan the walkthroughs.

Start by creating a simple list of tasks for the feature. These should be the core tasks required to configure a feature or set of features. For example, if your application is used for booking tickets to movies, and you are testing the seat selection options in reservation workflows, your main task list may look something like this:

- The users will enter the application and navigate to the movie of their choice.
- The users will reserve tickets and navigate to the seat selection tool.
- The users will use the seat map to select seats.
- The users will change the seat selection.
- The users will add a seat to their reserved seats.
- The users will cancel a seat.

Create a story for each task or for the set of tasks. This is what the participant will use throughout the session. For example, using the tasks above, you would write something like:

You are ordering tickets for the movie *Star Wars 5* for yourself and three friends.

1. Order your tickets and the seats. You would like to sit in the middle section of the theater, in the VIP seats.
2. Now a friend has asked to join you. Instead of three tickets, you need four.
3. Your friends decided they don't want to pay extra for their seats and ask you to change the seating to the row behind the VIP seats.

Unfortunately, two friends have to attend another event that evening. You need to reduce the number of seats to two.

Notice that the tasks don't use terminology that would be found in the application. The user must surmise from the tasks what options they are looking for.

1. Create the master document for the sessions. This includes the tasks you identified and the expected user workflow. This should also have a place for recording your observations and the user actions.
2. Choose and schedule your participants. Again, three to five will be enough per feature. Later, when you test the entire workflow, you may want to invite five to eight participants. Allow one to two hours for each session, depending on the complexity of the feature and the number of tasks the user will be asked to complete.

Running the Feature Walkthrough

When your task list is ready and the infrastructure for running the evaluation is prepared, you are ready to schedule the sessions.

1. Schedule at least one team member, such as the designer, developer, or project manager, to attend each session. This person should have some

understanding of the feature. While it's important to have another teammate with you, only one person should talk to the participants during the session. Make this clear to any observers. Otherwise the session may lose focus, and the participants may go off-task with questions and comments from the team.

2. Make sure that the atmosphere is friendly and inviting, and that you are all set up when the participants arrive. If the participants are not from your company, you may need them to sign a nondisclosure agreement.

3. Explain to the participants the overall purpose of the application and of the features they are evaluating. Remind them that you are looking for feedback and that they should talk out loud during the session so that you can understand what they are thinking.

4. Have the participants take a few minutes to simply look at the page and tell you what they would do first on the page. This lets you know what catches their eye on first glance.

5. Have the participants complete each task. If they appear uncertain about something, it's okay to ask them what they are thinking. However, try to keep the interruptions to a minimum; instead listen to what they are saying. Be sure to take notes and write down your observations.

6. After the participants complete the task, ask them for comments, or any other feedback you may find useful. You can ask them what they liked or didn't like about the feature, or how it compares to other applications they use.

After the Evaluation

1. Review the feedback from all the walkthroughs to look for similarities and differences. Based on your analysis of the participants' comments and the trends you discovered, decide how you can improve the terminology, information flow, text, labels, and the like.

2. Create a list of issues and suggested fixes for the issues. This may require you to meet with your product team or UX designer to find ways to change the information flow or deal with any other issues that came up during the walkthroughs.

Feature walkthroughs are a fun and valuable source of feedback that can be conducted throughout the design and development process. Feature walkthroughs early in the design cycle can help you define the information experience and content users will need. When done later in the development cycle, they are a good tool for helping you refine the content and text. Keep in mind, however, that at each milestone and phase in the development cycle, changes to the user interface infrastructure become more difficult.

Usability Studies

Formal usability studies became popular for investigating human—computer interaction in the 1980s. Since then, usability as a profession has sky-rocketed, with numerous institutions offering degrees leading to usability professions.

Formal usability studies are a powerful tool for identifying usability issues within an application and for testing user experiences. In this context, they are also useful for identifying and fixing issues in the integrated information experience. Perhaps the biggest downside of formal usability studies is the amount of planning involved and the high expenses incurred. Renting a usability lab and hiring a usability professional are useful, and at least one formal usability study during the product design is highly recommended. If your team decides to invest in a formal usability study, numerous books, web sites, and professional consultants are available that will help you set it up and run the sessions.

Regardless of your team's decision to invest in a formal usability test, you can also run your own informal usability study with support from your team. The main difference between this type of evaluation method and a feature walkthrough is that you will also test how the users move between features and how they perceive the application as a whole, rather than feature by feature.

Testing the information experience in this way provides insight into how users understand the information per feature, and also into the connection between features, the navigation model, and all the content presented along the way. Unlike the case for other methods, in usability testing (formal or informal) you will want your participants to match your target audience as closely as possible. This means recruiting people outside of your organization. It's amazing what people are willing to do to get a chance to make an impact on a new product. Offering a small gratuity for a few hours of someone's time seems to be all that is required.

Planning the Usability Study

Similar to other methods described earlier, the first task is to decide on the activities the user is going to complete. This doesn't just include a task-by-task list, but also the connection between tasks.

1. Start by creating a simple list of tasks. These should be the core tasks required to configure the main features in the application. For example, if your application is used for a tracking exercise and diet, you may have a list with these kinds of tasks:
   - The user will create the user profile.

- The user will set a goal weight.
- The user will calculate exercise and diet needs to meet the goal weight.
- The user will set the activity profile.
- The user will enter diet preferences.
- The user will track dietary intake.
- The user will track daily exercise output.
- The user will set a weekly schedule for exercise.
- The user will define a weekly schedule for diet.

2. Create the story for each task or set of tasks. This is what the participant will use throughout the session. For example, using the tasks above, you would write something like:

You have just downloaded a new a diet and exercise application from the Internet. Your friend Tom wants to see how it works. So, you offer to help him get started. His current weight is 160, but he wants to weigh 130. Tom is 25 years old.

- Fill in Tom's current details.

- Help Tom create an exercise program to reach his goal weight in 4 weeks. His calorie intake should be 1500 calories per day.

These are the foods Tom regularly eats during the day; help him fill in a daily diet.

Notice that the exercises are task-based, not feature-based. We don't tell the user to click the user profile option or select the exercise program option. The user must surmise which options to select based on the text and options presented in the user interface.

1. Create the master document for the sessions. This includes the tasks you identified and the expected user workflow. This should also have a place for recording your observations and the user actions.
2. Choose and schedule people to participate. Even three to five participants are enough to see trends develop and find the main glitches or areas that need improvement. Allow one to two hours for each session, depending on the complexity of the feature and the number of tasks the user will be asked to complete.

Running the Study

When your task list is ready and the infrastructure for running the evaluation is prepared, you are ready to schedule the sessions. Think about how you want to run the sessions. It's a good idea to get the team as involved as possible: observing the sessions, or talking to the participant afterward.

1. Schedule at least one team member, such as the designer, developer, or project manager, to attend each session. This person should have some understanding of the feature. While it's important to have another teammate with you, make it clear to any observers that only one person should talk to the participants during the session. Otherwise the session may lose focus, and the participants may go off-task with questions and comments from the team.
2. Make sure that the atmosphere is friendly and inviting and that you are all set up when the participants arrive. If the participants are not from your company, you may need them to sign a nondisclosure agreement.
3. Explain to the participants the overall purpose of the application. Remind them that you are looking for feedback and that they should talk out loud during the session so that you can understand what they are thinking. Thank them for participating, and remind them that they are not being tested: It is the design that you are testing.
4. Have the participants take a few minutes to simply look at the page and tell you what they would do first on the page. This lets you know what catches their eye on first glance.
5. Have the participants complete each task. If they appear uncertain about something, it's okay to ask them what they are thinking. However, try to keep the interruptions to a minimum; instead listen to what they are saying. Be sure to take notes and write down your observations.
6. After the participants complete the task, ask them for comments or any other feedback you may find useful. You can ask them what they liked or didn't like about the feature, or how it compares to other applications they use. You may want to provide a short survey about the workflow and options.

After the Evaluation

1. Review the feedback from all the participants to identify similarities and differences in what they said and did. Based on your analysis of the participants' comments and the trends you discovered, decide how you can improve the terminology, information flow, text, labels, and so on.
2. Create a list of issues and suggested fixes for the issues. This may require you to meet with your product team or UX designer to find ways to change the information flow, or deal with any other issues that came up during the walkthroughs.

Usability studies are a valuable tool. Whenever possible, get the team involved in watching the study, and invite the main stakeholder in to talk to the participants after the study. When done later on in the development cycle, they are a good tool for helping you refine the content and text.

Keep in mind, however, that at each milestone and phase in the development cycle, changes to the user interface infrastructure become more difficult.

SUMMARY

Regardless of how well you have planned, designed, and created your information experience, and each string of text comprising the experience, the final step is to verify the information. Without verification, you have no way of measuring how well you have met the information needs of your users.

- Verifying the information experience includes validating the clarity, consistency, and accuracy of your information.
- After creating your text, plan a team review with key members of the team to get their feedback. The earlier you do this in the process, the better it is for getting changes made.
- You can use a variety of methods to validate the information experience, including heuristic evaluations, feature walkthroughs, and usability studies.
- Before creating your task list for an evaluation, create a list of five to ten heuristics you want to assess. Then build your task list accordingly.
- After validating the information experience, prioritize the issues that were observed and present your recommendations to the team.

Review Check List

Basic Rules

1. Understand your users. What level of knowledge is expected? Try to sit in the customer chair's, and see if everything makes sense and is friendly.
2. Provide enough information for users to make an informed choice. Language should be appropriate and consistent throughout. But don't overload the UI with text.
3. Pages should be well organized. Spacing and alignment should indicate the workflow. Controls and options should be grouped logically so that it's clear what items belong together.
4. Controls should be intuitive and provide meaning. For example, don't let the user select an item from an empty list; don't use acronyms that the user might not understand.
5. Text should be clearly written. There should be no spelling mistakes, typos, or grammatical errors.

General UI Review

1. Default values are provided and appropriate.
2. The default option is the recommended option and is listed first (where applicable).
3. Unit is appropriate for the input (e.g., 60,000 seconds is expressed in minutes, and it should be clear to the user). Units should appear in parentheses as part of the text. Example: "Timeout limit (minutes):"
4. Input fields are sized according to expected user input. This provides a visual cue as to the expected values that may be entered. For example, if the string the user will enter is a number between 0 and 999, restrict the user from entering strings exceeding three characters or containing nonnumeric characters.
5. If control text is not self-explanatory, then an explanation, or help link to an explanation, is provided.

6. Examples are provided, and appropriate as needed. For example, if the user must enter a URL, an example using the correct URL format displays under the text box.
7. Right-click menus are included, in the correct order; match the corresponding task if provided elsewhere, such as in a tasks pane.
8. Menus and buttons opening a dialog should end with "…". If the action is triggered immediately when clicking the button, no … is used. Examples [Add …], [Delete]
9. Button names, menu items, and dialog title bars are written in title case, or sentence case (just be consistent).
10. Controls are written in sentence case without ending punctuation.

Dialogs and Wizards

11. UI focus is on the correct control.
12. UI validation blocks users from misconfiguring the feature.
13. Page titles match page functionality. If launched from a button, the title reflects the button label.
14. Controls are the standard sizes.
15. Text is aligned properly (usually aligned left).
16. Radio buttons and checkbox controls are aligned appropriately with the control text (top, left). This is particularly important when the text wraps.
17. Button labels are appropriate (e.g., "Add" versus "New," "Delete" versus "Remove.")
18. Pages and controls are spaced appropriately so that the user can easily see the relationship between the controls (no large gaps, not too close together). If the page is being localized, remember to leave 30 percent extra line space for localization.
19. Subordinate controls are indented under the superior control, and are grayed out until relevant.
20. Defaults change according to previous selections, and invalid selections are grayed out.
21. Property sheets and wizard pages are sized correctly and consistently throughout the product.
22. If additional steps are required after leaving the wizard or dialog, the user is notified of such steps.

Validation

23. **Validate!** Make sure that you validate all user input fields.
24. Users cannot move to the next wizard page if parameters are wrong or missing.
25. All errors are handled, and a message is provided.

26. Validation messages are appropriate and helpful. For example, "Invalid port range" is not a good message. A better message is: "The specified port range is invalid. A valid port range cannot exceed 65535."

Popup Messages

27. Page title is correct. That is, the page title depends on the page from which the message is launched.
28. Message is clearly written, and the expected user action is obvious from the text. Buttons should match the text. (Most cases use OK/Cancel. Only use Yes/No where required.)
29. Icons are used correctly (warnings, Info, Help, Error).

Help Links

30. Help links are active and link to the correct topic.
31. Inline help links are consistently presented, as determined by your team guidelines.

Localization

32. Leave 30 percent extra line space for localization (this is relevant for all pages that will be localized).

Accessibility (Hotkeys, Tabs)

33. Tab order is correct: top to bottom, left to right.
34. Each control has a distinct access key. In the wizard page, the N and B letters are used by the Next and Back buttons, respectively, and should not be used within the page. The same is true for the A letter in property pages, where it is being used by the Apply button.
35. Access keys are assigned to visible (thick) letters. Do not use I, l, j, p, t, i.
36. No access keys are assigned for OK, Finish, Cancel, or Help command buttons because OK and Finish are assigned the function of ENTER, Cancel is assigned the function of ESC, and Help is assigned the function of F1. Make sure that these keys work for dialog boxes.

Alerts and Events

37. Alert names and definitions are appropriate for the alert action.

Error Messages (Event Viewer)

38. Error text is clearly written.
39. Error message tells the user what happened to cause the error and provides possible user actions to fix the problem.

Final Summary

The strategies and processes described in this book are meant to help you understand how to create an information experience that moves your customers successfully through the tasks and workflows provided in your application. A positive information experience makes for happy customers, and happy customers are what ultimately keep companies in business.

While it's not always possible to follow a process from start to finish, properly going through each step, let's review the stages that were presented in this book, as a reminder of the goals and objectives of each stage, as they were outlined in each of the sections.

Section 1 (Chapters 1–2): In this section you learned about the components of an information ecosystem and information experience. You also learned about how teams create software, the benefits and drawbacks of different design models, and how the role and tasks of the information designer fit into the design process of the team.

Section 3 (Chapters 3, 4, 5): In this section you learned how to gather data and identify the different types of users interacting with your application, and how the needs of the user depend on a variety of factors, such as user tasks, user knowledge levels, and demographics. You learned how to gather and analyze data about your users. In Chapter 5 you learned how to create a tasks list and map the list to create personas and persona biographies.

Section 3 (Chapters 6, 7, 8): In these chapters you learned how users read online and how to design the information experience based on user reading patterns and usability principles. You also learned about creating content guidelines and strategies for selecting content types that are appropriate for the needs of your users.

Section 4 (Chapters 9, 10, 11): In this section you learned about implementing the content your users will interact with while using your application. This included designing your text, developing strategies for writing the content, and producing content for diverse audiences.

Section 5 (Chapter 12): This section described the methods for evaluating the information within the user interface, using common usability methods, such as heuristic walkthroughs. The end of the section includes a check list for reviewing your information and content.

Wishing you much success designing and creating the content and information your users need to successfully and happily use your applications.

Bibliography

Clicktale.com, ClickTale Ltd, 2012.

Cooper, A., Reinmann, R., & Cronin, D. (2007). *About face 3: The essentials of interaction design.* Hoboken, NJ: John Wiley and Sons.

Flemming, M. L., & Levie, W. H. (1984). *Instructional message design.* Educational Design Publications, Inc.

Gunther-Danierl, R. *Neuronale netze eine einführung.* Universitat Wurzburg.

Microsoft Corporation. (2010). *Windows user experience interaction guidelines (UX Guide) for windows 7 and windows vista.*

Nielsen, J. (2006). *Eyetracking web usability.* New Riders Press.

Nielson, J. (2007). Useit.com by Jakob Nielsen.

Sharif, B., & Maletic, J. I. *An eye tracking study on the effects of layout in understanding the role of design patterns.* Department of Computer Science, Kent State University.

Strunk, W., Jr. (1999). *The elements of style.* New York: Bartleby.Com. Tobii.com. Eye Tracking and Gaze Interaction by Tobii Technology. Tobii Technology AB.

U.S. Department of Health and Human Services (2006). *The research-based web design & usability guidelines* (Enlarged/Expanded edition). Washington, DC: U.S. Government Printing Office.

Index

Related Titles from Morgan Kaufmann

Designing the Search Experience
The Information Architecture of Discovery
Tony Russell-Rose and Tyler Tate
978012396981

Data Insights
New Ways to Visualize and Make Sense of Data
Hunter Whitney
9780123877932

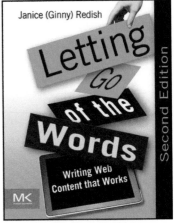

Letting Go of the Words, 2nd Edition
Writing Web Content that Works
Janice (Ginny) Redish
9780123859303

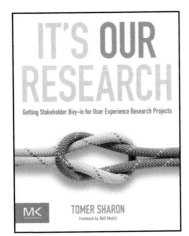

It's our Research
Getting Stakeholder Buy-in for User Experience Research Projects
Tomer Sharon
9780123851307

Usability Testing Essentials
Ready, Set...Test!
Carol M. Barnum
9780123750921

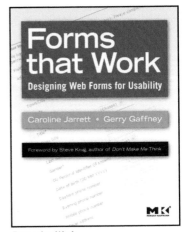

Forms that Work
Designing Web Forms for Usability
Caroline Jarrett and Gerry Gaffney
9781558607101

mkp.com

Printed and bound by CPI Group (UK) Ltd, Croydon, CR0 4YY

03/10/2024

01040318-0001